THE CRUISE TRAVELER'S HANDBOOK

How to find and enjoy unforgettable cruise vacations

Gary Bembridge

The Cruise Traveler's Handbook: how to find and enjoy unforgettable cruise vacations

Library and Archives Canada Cataloguing in Publication

Bembridge, Gary, 1959-, author
The cruise traveler's handbook : how to find and enjoy unforgettable cruise vacations / Gary Bembridge.

ISBN 978-1-927557-04-4

1. Cruise lines--Handbooks, manuals, etc. 2. Cruise ships--Handbooks, manuals, etc. 3. Ocean travel--Handbooks, manuals, etc. 4. Vacations--Handbooks, manuals, etc. I. Title.

G550.B44 2013 910.2'02 C2013-905173-2
C2013-905174-0

Disclaimer:

This book provides entertaining and informative snapshots of the writer's personal experiences while cruising, as well as anecdotes from other travelers. The Cruise Traveler's Handbook is not meant to serve as an exclusive checklist to effectively safeguard the reader in every travel or cruising situation, and is sold with the understanding that neither the author nor the publisher intend to render any type of medical, legal, or professional advice. No one can guarantee safety and travel can expose everyone to potential risks. Because safety is impacted by each person's actions and choices, each reader assumes all responsibilities and obligations with respect to any decisions made as a result of the use of any content in this book. While all reasonable measures have been taken to ensure the quality, reliability, and accuracy of the information in the Cruise Traveler's Handbook, author and publisher make no warranties or guarantees, expressed or implied, by including providing content in this book. Any implied warranties of merchantability or fitness of use for a particular purpose are also disclaimed. Neither the author or publisher, nor any contributor, will be liable for damages arising out of or in connection with the use of The Cruise Traveler's Handbook. Because of the dynamic nature of online media, certain web addresses or links contained in this book may have changed since publication and may no longer be valid.

To My Dad,
Philip Henry Green Bembridge,
who was always so proud of everything I did.

He would never have stopped telling everyone about
his son writing this book.

Acknowledgements

More than anybody in the world, I thank Mark, my partner of more than a decade. Despite suffering from seasickness, he embraced my love of cruising. Mark always supports me in everything I do, and has been with me through the many good times. Even more importantly, he gave me the strength to survive through the tough times, too.

I also want to thank the people who read the manuscript in its various stages, and gave their input and ideas, and whose comments have helped me craft a better book. Specifically, I want to thank Mark, Gordon Mundie, Jane Chadwick and Tom Mullen.

A special thanks also to my fellow cruising fans who keep me entertained and informed all year round through their blogs, and who also contributed stories to the book.

And finally, I want to acknowledge the people who work so hard to make cruising possible. They work long and incredibly hard hours with passion and a smile.

Table of Contents

Table of Contents

The Backstory: Cruising and Me

Before I stepped on board a cruise ship for the first time, I had thought cruising would make me feel trapped, would be too regimented, and was probably really only for old people anyway. I had no desire to cruise, and dismissed this fabulous vacation option out of hand. I wish I had been more inquisitive earlier.

I stumbled into cruising through work. I was invited to attend a three-day marketing conference on a cruise ship. With my feelings about cruising already set, I was focused on the content of the conference and not on the experience of being on a ship.

However, as we sailed down the Solent River from Southampton and entered the English Channel, I was surprised to find myself overcome with emotion. I was experiencing something magical. The sense of heading out to sea on a massive ship as it churned through the ocean was exciting. Feeling the gentle movement as it carved its way through the sea, leaving land and the glimmering lights of the city behind, I was elated. Watching the waves crashing against the hull was mesmerizing. At that moment, I truly appreciated what cruising is about.

For me, cruising is like an advent calendar in the run-up to Christmas. Each morning, I look forward to pulling back the curtains to see what new delight is revealed. On a land-based holiday, no matter how beautiful the view from my hotel, I am always a little disappointed to find it is the same one I left behind the night before.

Cruising is perfect for my approach to travel, which is to see as much as I can, while I can. I believe this was influenced by my experiences growing up in Zimbabwe. During my boyhood and teen years, I lived through a civil war that took many lives. I grew up with an appreciation that life is precious and limited, and so you must make the most of every day. Every year, my family would go on a seaside holiday in or around Durban, South Africa. It was a long drive that took almost three full days in the car, with no sightseeing on the way. Of course, Zimbabwe and South Africa are fascinating places, but as a child I was convinced that places I had not visited were better than those I had. I still hold that belief. I am driven to see as many new things as I can, in as little time as possible.

My first major cruise was a transatlantic crossing in the middle of winter. People warned me that it was madness, as the North Atlantic in winter can be a vicious beast. It was incredible. Fifty-foot waves crashed over the bow of the ship. Taking stairs required moving in time with the movement of the sea. The cabin creaked constantly, and at night we removed the drawers from the bedside table to prevent them from slamming open and shut. As we eventually sailed past the Statue of Liberty to dock in Manhattan, the Hudson River was calm and welcoming and despite my rough adventure, I knew I had totally fallen in love with cruising.

Cruising has taken me to places I would never have considered going, and has led me to experience things I would otherwise never have tried. When I discovered cruising as a vacation, it immediately felt comfortable. It satisfies my desire to keep going to new places, and it feeds me new scenery, destinations, and attractions to explore every day. Cruising is more than a journey. It keeps serving up tasty samples of the world and I love it.

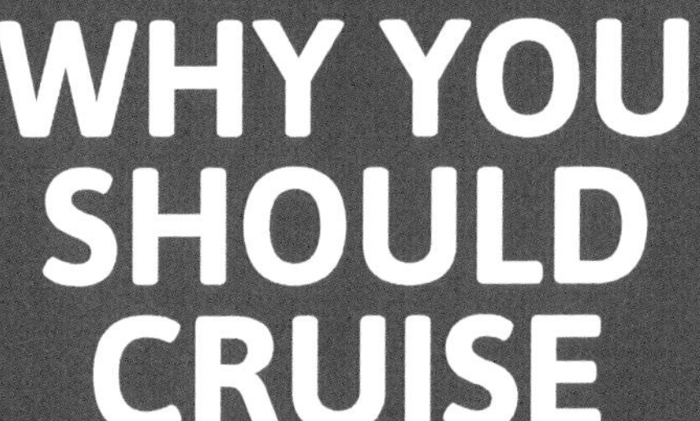

"Airplane travel is nature's way of making you look like your passport photo"

Al Gore

Dominica is one of my favorite islands in the Caribbean. As it does not have a long runway suitable for large airliners, cruising makes it easier to visit.

Who Is the Cruise Traveler's Handbook For?

More than three quarters of the earth is covered in water. Using it to explore our fascinating world is what this book is about.

Over the centuries, access to water has determined where people settle and build villages that grow into towns and sometimes turn into vast, sprawling cities. Getting to these destinations by water allows you to enjoy every minute of your journey, without the hassle and stress of airports and traffic. Waterways also deliver you into the heart of a destination, close to where its most interesting attractions and sights are located.

It's important to note that cruising is much more than large passenger cruise ships. This handbook looks at all the ways to explore the world from the water. As you read further, you will discover there are many.

What Cruising Means to a 23-Year-Old

Emma Gray blogs at EmmaOnBoard.com

Whenever I tell someone that I'm heading off on yet another cruise holiday, I notice a furrow of the brow, and the look of surprise that creeps onto their face. I know they're questioning why a 23-year-old woman would be going on the type of holiday they associate with middle aged people with money.

These misconceptions couldn't be further from reality. The average age of cruise passengers is dropping, and now you're likely to end up on a ship surrounded by young couples, friends and families.

In the last ten years I've been lucky enough to take 14 different cruises with seven different cruise lines. Just what is it that keeps me going back?

I have an unquenchable thirst for travel. Waking up in a new place almost every day of my holiday is one of the main factors that attracted me to cruising in the beginning, and keeps me returning. There are also a multitude of things to do on board and the opportunity to meet new people of all ages, backgrounds, and nationalities. It's no wonder I've become hooked.

With everyone quite literally being in the same boat, most cruise passengers are very friendly. This makes it easy to strike up new friendships on board. After a day of exploring a new destination, I love to return to the ship to share dinner or a cocktail with my new friends, and hear how they spent their day.

Some of my favorite cruise memories are from a Mediterranean voyage I embarked upon in my late teens. I have vivid recollections of waking up, excited to be in a new port of call. I enjoy soaking up the culture and sampling the local flavors, before getting back on board and preparing for an evening of fun. I ended most nights of that voyage in the ship's lively nightclub – dancing, laughing, and having the time of my life with people my own age.

As a young female, safety is also one of the major advantages of cruising. If I stay out late, I don't have to worry about getting home safely – as I might have to do in a holiday resort or when visiting a foreign city. I simply take the nearest elevator back to my stateroom. Then I can collapse on my bed for some well-earned rest and get ready to tackle a new day of exploration on land.

For me, cruising is a great way to travel, and I hope to continue clocking up the nights on board for many years to come.

Cruising Myths Dispelled

Let's start by getting rid of some of the myths and concerns about cruising. As Emma has shown, it's not just for the old. And if you think it's not for you because you get seasick – well, you should think again.

Let's dispel some myths before exploring how to find and enjoy unforgettable cruise vacations.

Seasickness

Anyone who has experienced seasickness knows it's miserable. Here are some of the ways that cruise companies minimize this risk:

- Routes are selected to limit the chances of hitting rough seas.
- Modern radar and navigation systems allow the Captain to set a course to avoid rough water.
- Stabilizers are used in large passenger ships to hold the ship steady, and prevent the side-to-side rocking motion that can cause seasickness.
- Cruises are scheduled when the sea is likely to be calm. Caribbean and Mediterranean cruises run during seasons when seas are more settled. River cruises sail on routes where there is little chance of becoming seasick.

If you are prone to seasickness, here's what you can do:

- Be positive. Do not convince yourself you are going to be seasick even before you have embarked on your cruise.
- Book a cabin in the middle of the ship and low down. When in the public areas of the ship, try to stay in the middle where there is the least movement.
- Use over-the-counter motion sickness pills. The most common pills include dimenhydrinate[1] (marketed as Dramamine, Gravol, etc.) in North America and cinnarazine[2] (marketed as Stugeron or Stunarone) in Europe. You must buy them before you go. They do have some side effects, such as drowsiness, but are very effective at preventing motion sickness for most people.

- If you get seasick on board, visit the medical center for an injection. You will sleep for a few hours, and then feel great. They will often also give you pills with the same active ingredient (promethazine) to take for the next few days.
- Eat ginger, drink ginger ale, get fresh air, and look at the horizon if you do have bouts of feeling queasy.

Only for Old People

Cruising has a reputation for having an older passenger mix. However, the demographics of passengers on a cruise will vary greatly based on the region of the world, the itinerary, and the cruise line. For example, it is possible to cruise around the Caribbean on the following:

- Fun boat of 20- and 30-somethings, dressed in shorts and t-shirts.
- Cultural cruise of people exploring history and food.
- Formal cruise, full of couples, with much dressing up.
- Disney cruise, full of families with young children.

The key is choosing the cruise type and line that best matches your interests, to ensure your fellow passengers are similar to you in age and passions.

Norovirus

This is a form of gastrointestinal illness that causes nausea, vomiting, and diarrhea. Symptoms can also include headaches, fever, and stomach cramps. It is contagious and spreads easily through touch. It is also common on land, but outbreaks are more obvious when they occur in the contained environment of a ship. Outbreaks are very infrequent, but well publicized when they occur.

Preventing norovirus is a priority on board. It is managed by:

- Requiring passengers to sign a declaration that they have not suffered from vomiting or diarrhea for 48 hours before boarding.
- Encouraging passengers to wash their hands frequently with soap and water, and to use the alcohol gel available around the ship.
- Enforcing strict cleansing protocols to sanitize handrails, elevator buttons, and other equipment handled frequently by passengers.

- Regular and unannounced on-board checks by the United Kingdom and United States vessel sanitation authorities.

Getting Bored

Boredom is rarely a problem. Most people I have met returning from a cruise complain that they did not have enough time to do everything they wanted. Cruise lines are experienced at ensuring that passengers have activities, events, and attractions to keep them busy.

The key to preventing boredom is selecting the right cruise that meets your needs. For example:

- If you need a wide choice of activities and facilities to keep you busy all day and night, you will prefer mega, resort-style passenger ships.
- If you enjoy long peaceful days reading or pursuing your hobby, then freighter cruising may be better for you.
- If you prefer being physically active, taking hikes, or cycling, a barge cruise along the canals of Europe allows for this.
- If listening to talks about the region and ports of call interests you, then a river cruise may be best.

Feeling Trapped

When people have never been on a cruise, they worry about feeling confined on a ship surrounded by water. However, ships usually cruise at night, and spend daytime hours in ports, thus reducing the chance you will feel trapped. Here are some suggestions for overcoming this fear:

- Arrange to go on a tour of the ship, or book onto a short two-night taster cruise, before making a commitment. This will give you a feel for the size, scale, and space.
- Take your first cruise with an itinerary that guarantees many opportunities to be on land. For example a passenger cruise ship that has port stops every day, or a river or barge cruise, as they stop frequently during the day and sail close to land.
- Do not take a transatlantic crossing as your first cruise. Seven days at sea may be too much for your first time out.

Accidents and Safety

Cruising accidents are relatively rare. While the media is more likely to highlight the risk of major accidents, such as the 2012 Costa Concordia accident (where the ship hit a rock and partially sank, which resulted in more than 30 deaths), passengers are more likely to experience incidents such as theft and assault[3]. You need to be aware and careful on a cruise, just as you would on any vacation when you are with groups of strangers, and visiting new and unfamiliar places.

In the last chapter of this book there is advice and tips about safety on board.

Tender boats are used to ferry passengers onto land when the ship cannot dock.

The Advantages of Cruising

There are many advantages to cruising compared to land-based vacations:

- You only need to pack and unpack once.
- Your transit time is also a part of the vacation.
- You can visit places that are difficult to access by land, such as Alaska, and the Norwegian Fjords.
- You can get an overview of a region without investing all your time and money into one destination.
- You can relax completely.

Trips that can only be done on a cruise

In some cases, cruising is your only option, as there are destinations that can be reached only by ship.

Transatlantic Crossing

Until the launch of scheduled non-stop jetliner travel in 1958, the only way to cross the Atlantic was by ocean liner. Jet planes wiped out this service when passengers switched to flights of around seven hours, as opposed to ocean crossings taking up to seven days. You can still cross the Atlantic by ship, but your choices are limited to scheduled summer crossings on Cunard's *Queen Mary 2*, freighters, or when cruise lines are repositioning their ships at the start and end of summer and winter seasons in Europe and the Caribbean/South America.

Transiting through the Panama Canal

This 100-year-old canal in Central America is a series of man-made locks and lakes that allow ships to pass from the Atlantic Ocean into the Pacific Ocean, without having to sail all the way around South America. The locks transport ships 85 feet above sea level, and then back down to sea level again. It takes a day to pass through the Panama Canal.

Transiting through the Suez Canal

This man-made canal connects the Mediterranean Sea to the Red Sea, and runs through Egypt. It was built to transport goods from the Far East to Europe, without having to navigate all the way around Africa. It is more than 100 miles long and, unlike the Panama Canal, does not require locks to enable ships to pass through. It has salt water flowing through it, and can handle large ships, including aircraft carriers and tankers.

Places where planes don't regularly fly

Saint Helena

Until 2016, when an airport will operate on the island, the only way to get to Saint Helena (off the west coast of Africa) is on a supply ship, the RMS Saint Helena. This ship sails from Cape Town, carrying passengers and goods for the island. It then sails on to the Ascension Islands, which are served by the UK's Royal Air Force flights, which can take limited numbers of civilian passengers.

Antarctica and the Arctic

The most common way to visit either region is by ship. These specialist ships, often with reinforced icebreaker hulls, are usually operated by independent exploration companies. As interest in seeing new and more unusual places has grown, some mainstream cruise lines have started to introduce dedicated ships designed for exploring these regions.

Galapagos Islands

This small and remote group of islands is 620 miles west of South America in the Pacific Ocean, and belongs to Ecuador. The islands are spread across an area of 19,500 square miles. They were made famous by Charles Darwin, who developed much of his theory of evolution based on his studies on the islands. Although you can fly into some of the bigger islands, you have to cruise to explore them. Licenses to run cruises are controlled, to help preserve the ecosystem, and are given mostly to independent yacht cruise operators.

Sailing into Sydney, past the Opera House, is a highlight of many world cruises.

Who is Suited to Cruising?

While there is a cruise for everyone, there are ten types of people for whom cruising is especially well suited.

1. **People who fear, or want to avoid, flying.**
   The ability to cruise from port to port means you can travel on vacation to and from a port close to you, avoiding the need to fly. Cruising even gives you the ability to completely circumnavigate the world without stepping onto a plane.

2. **Resort vacation lovers.**
   If you enjoy going to resorts, you will like many types of cruises. Even on smaller cruise ships with around 200–300 passengers, there are restaurants, bars, entertainment venues, daily activities, shops, swimming pools, spas, and fitness centers. Larger cruise ships have more ambitious resort-like attractions, such as water slides, rock-climbing walls, ice rinks, bowling alleys, 3-D simulator rides, and outdoor cinemas.

3. **Families with children and babies.**
   Most cruise lines welcome and cater to families by running kids' clubs and teen clubs to provide supervised play and activities during the day. Many also offer babysitting services in the evenings. Many families like the security of cruising, as they know their children will be supervised throughout the day and restricted to the confines of the ship so they cannot wander off. Cruising gives parents the ability to enjoy time for themselves.

4. **Cross-generation holiday makers.**
   A growing trend on cruises is multi-generational or extended family groups traveling together. The diversity of on-board activities, the variety of excursions to suit different interests, and the range of cabins to accommodate different budgets and group sizes makes it possible to travel as a family on one ship without a lot of compromises. Each

member of the family can pursue his or her own interests through the day, go on excursions that satisfy individual interests and activity levels, and stay in budget-appropriate cabins while still sharing meals and other major events such as the evening shows.

5. **Seniors.**
Cruising has always been popular with seniors. It provides a way to keep exploring the world in an organized, relatively stress-free and safe manner. You don't have to navigate through airports, find your way through strange towns, or find suitable, safe, and comfortable accommodation.

Cruise lines also cater to the needs of senior travelers by offering escorted excursions with limited walking, and arranging activities to meet mature passenger interests. There is also the reassurance of having an on-board medical facility to deal with health issues, thereby avoiding the challenges of navigating an unfamiliar medical system.

6. **People getting married, honeymooning, or renewing their vows.**
It is possible to get married or renew your vows on many cruise ships. It gives you a chance to combine your wedding, celebration, and honeymoon in one activity. The romance and relative uniqueness of being married at sea makes it an ideal alternative to traditional church or civil ceremony weddings.

For the Captain to perform the legal marriage ceremony, the ship has to be registered in a country that allows such services. Your travel agent can confirm whether this is possible.

7. **Solo Travelers.**
Most types of cruises cater to solo travelers, and ensure they feel welcome and integrated.

The lifestyle on cruises makes it easy for solo travelers to meet people and not feel isolated. Cruise travelers are friendly and eager to strike up conversations with other passengers. Cruises are organized to encourage interaction, especially at mealtimes. Most types of cruises host daily informal events for solo travelers to get together, and some bigger ocean cruise lines have male dance hosts available in the ballroom to partner with female solo travelers.

Many of the new large cruise ships have dedicated solo cabins. Booking a solo cabin means you can avoid the surcharge, often referred to as a 'single supplement', levied for single occupancy. Some cruise lines will help you find a roommate to share costs, or you can use cruise message boards to find suitable cabin mates.

River cruises have always enthusiastically embraced solo travel, and most offer no-penalty solo travel fares as standard, while others run promotions removing solo travel surcharges on selected cruises.

8. **Disabled, Special Needs, and Mobility Restricted Travelers.** Freighters, yachts, barges, and most river cruise boats are not suitable for disabled passengers. However, many of the newer ocean cruise ships are suited for passengers who have special needs or mobility issues, and include the following features:

- mobility-restricted access cabins with suitable bathroom facilities, and cupboards designed for people to use and access from wheelchairs.
- passageways, decks, and public areas designed for wheelchair access; modern ships also have automatic doors to access outside areas.
- theaters with dedicated areas for wheelchair passengers and their companions.
- lifting equipment to enable mobility-restricted passengers to enter the pool.
- ramps to get on and off the ship at embarkation and disembarkation points, with crew on-hand to assist.
- a medical center with doctors and nurses on call to deal with issues 24 hours a day, although there is a charge for using these services.

The 'Resources' section lists companies that can give advice, offer items for hire, and install the mobility equipment you may need while on board.

Discuss with the cruise agent and the cruise line if the ship you are considering is suitable. Cruise message boards online are also a good source of information.

9. **People with Special Interests and Hobbies.**

   Themed cruises are a growing trend: cruise lines are organizing more of them, allowing promoters and groups to charter ships for specific themes, and permitting parties to make block bookings on selected cruises.

   There is a themed cruise for almost every topic you can think of, and the website Theme Cruise Finder (themecruisefinder.com) usually has at least 500 different options listed at any one time.

10. **You!**

    Even if you do not fall into any of these groups, I believe there is a cruise option and ship type that will meet your requirements.

    Through the course of this book, I will explore the varied options. I am convinced that one of them will strike a chord and appeal to you.

130 miles inland at Skjolden, Norway, while cruising on the *Queen Elizabeth.*

The Reluctant River Cruiser

Janice Waugh blogs at SoloTravelerBlog.com

I'm a bit of a snob.

A reverse snob by most standards, but a snob nonetheless.

I generally like to travel on the cheap – low-to-the-ground so that I connect with locals and other travelers. I travel solo, and find expensive hotels to be impersonal as guests don't mingle and locals are a rarity. While I enjoy luxury when traveling for work, I have generally preferred to stay in B&Bs, hostels, and budget hotels when going for pleasure.

My first river cruise changed my thinking. I confess I'm a convert. This will not be my exclusive mode of travel, but it is certainly an option I'll enjoy again.

I boarded the ship at noon on a Sunday, and was greeted by a friendly crew. The rooms were not scheduled to be ready until two o'clock, but lunch was being served so I had my first taste of the food. With only 88 passengers on this sailing (and a capacity of about 120), the kitchen produced quality food equal to that of a fine restaurant. During the entire cruise, fresh ingredients were picked up along the way, and there was usually an aspect of each night's menu that reflected the local cuisine.

After lunch I checked in, and found my cabin where my bags had magically appeared. The bed was comfortable, the closets ample, and the bathroom beautiful. Having spent the previous week in hostels in London and Nuremberg, I admit that I was actually giddy. The luxury was welcome!

One of the best things about river cruising for a solo traveler is the opportunity to meet people. From the first afternoon, I met passengers from many countries. And because I intentionally sat with different people for dinner every night, and connected with others on the various free tours that were offered during the day, I got to hear their stories. On a river cruise, the intimate environment allows you to get to know many people.

Low-to-the-ground travel can be hard work. Figuring out logistics, booking your accommodation, finding a good place to eat, packing and unpacking... it's fun and rewarding but also challenging and tiring. River cruising is definitely an option for solo travelers like me, and I've decided, it fits with how I like to experience the world.

PLANNING YOUR CRUISE

"I have always found that plans are useless, but planning is indispensable"

Dwight D. Eisenhower

Meeting Wonderful People On Board is No Gamble

When I am in Las Vegas, I stick to the slot machines. The players at the tables are there strictly for gambling. They are obsessed with how you play, and blur into one characterless bank of people that does not reveal any personality or back story. The casino on a cruise ship is quite different, as the tables attract characters you want to meet, mix, and connect with.

One year, I spent three weeks on the *Queen Mary 2* over Christmas and New Year. There, our nightly games of blackjack became a social hub for a diverse bunch of people. I learned something from each and every one of them.

Our most unforgettable blackjack table friend was Vera. In the 1950s, she worked on the original *Queen Elizabeth*, as a hairdresser on the ship preparing film stars for the balls. She would hint at the names of the famous women she had styled, but we were all too young to know who they were.

Vera was well over 70, and wonderfully glamorous. She wore a different sparkling outfit every night. She sailed the Christmas voyage every year, entertaining everyone with her stories of working for those ladies who occupied the luxurious suites. Working with these glamorous ladies then drove Vera to set up her own business and, ultimately, she became one of those women herself. Her drive and ambition inspired me.

Next to Vera would sit the young 'Russian Guy'. He was traveling with his mother, who spoke no English. He never spoke to anyone. He would growl and tap his chips irritably when we did not play by the accepted rules of blackjack. But between his scowling and tapping, he would turn to his mother seated next to him and his face would soften. He would translate jokes, check that she was enjoying herself, order her a drink, and ask if she wanted to do something else. He was clearly taking her on a trip that had been a dream of hers, and he was making sure it was memorable for her. He made me feel I should be doing more for my mother.

We were joined at the table by 'The Boston Family', a couple traveling with their two children, and her parents. They would alternate on who was going to lose their money each night. Every time we saw them, they would tell me how their mother loved my blog and was dying to meet me. I never met her as she was always off doing something by herself, with the children, or with new friends she had met. It reinforced for me how the varied activities on a ship make it possible for multiple generations of families to travel together, while still allowing everyone to explore their individual interests.

Then there were the two large Americans we called 'The Jocks'. Tall, with bulging muscles, they looked full of aggression and testosterone. I assumed they would be loud, obnoxious, over-confident, and judgmental. They were the opposite. Every evening, they joined our table and politely listened to Vera's stories, smiled at the Russian Guy's mother, and asked what we had been doing. It reminded me of how quick I am to judge people by stereotypes, and how the shared experience of being on a ship at sea draws us together into a community.

It is this very sense of community, of shared time, space and purpose, which draws me to cruising. The power of being in one ship heading to a common destination causes people to mix and socialize. What a pity life on land is not a bit more like this.

The beautiful cathedral in Helsinki. I would never have visited if it had not been for cruising.

Main Cruising Options

When choosing a cruise vacation, you should first decide which type of cruise experience and cruise line will best meet your interests and needs. People accustomed to land-based vacations find this unusual, as they are accustomed to choosing where they want to go, and then deciding how to get there.

When cruising, the mode of travel is also your accommodation, the place you eat most of your meals, and where you will spend at least half of every day. The secret to an unforgettable cruising vacation is being clear about what form of cruising will suit you, and then deciding on the specific itinerary.

This section explores the range of cruise options available, including some of the more unusual and quirky.

Ocean Passenger Cruise Ships

There are three categories of passenger cruise ships.

Large Cruise Ships (sometimes called 'Mega Ships' or 'Resort Ships')

Large cruise ships carry between 1,750 and 6,500 passengers, and look like vast sailing apartment blocks. Due to the number of people needed to fill them, they operate in the popular cruise regions such as the Caribbean and the Mediterranean. They suit people who enjoy being in busy, bustling environments with lots going on and many choices.

Pros:

- There are many dining choices and venues.
- You will find resort-like attractions, including water-slides, bowling alleys, ice rinks, and climbing walls.
- You can enjoy big Las Vegas-style shows and Broadway musicals. Some ships even have water acrobatic shows.
- Large clubs for kids and teens are provided to meet the needs of the many families choosing to sail on these ships.

Cons:

- Due to the size and number of guests, procedures are regimented and rules less flexible.
- Service has to focus on speed and efficiency, so it can feel less personal.
- It takes longer to check in, board, and disembark.
- Ports of call are limited, due to the ship's size and the numbers of passengers a destination can handle. If tendering to land is required it can mean lengthy delays in ports.
- Fares are low to fill the ships, but they encourage additional on-board spending and have more add-on charges.

Mid-sized Cruise Ships

Mid-sized cruise ships carry between 750 and 1,750 passengers. The smaller size means they can visit a wider range of ports. They cruise in most regions around the world.

Pros:

- It is easier to find your way around, but the ships are still large enough to provide a choice of dining and entertainment venues.
- A wide range of accommodation is available, from large suites to inside cabins, to attract and appeal to broader audiences and budgets.
- They are better in rough seas than the large mega ships, as they are less 'top heavy'.
- There are fewer embarking and disembarking delays and lines, even in ports requiring tenders.
- Some cruise lines have adult-only ships, as they are able to fill ships of this size without having to appeal to a wide demographic audience.
- Service is more personal than on the large ships.

Cons:

- There will be less choice in dining venues, facilities, and entertainment than on the large 'mega ships'.
- They may have kid- and teen clubs, but they will likely be smaller than on the big cruise ships.

Small and 'Boutique' Cruise Ships

Small cruise ships carry between 250 and 750 passengers. While they cruise all the popular regions, they can call into ports that cannot handle mid-sized ships, so they can offer more unusual itineraries. Small cruise ships are positioned and priced as 'luxury' cruise lines due to their high service levels.

Pros:

- All-inclusive fares usually include items that the larger cruise ships charge extra for, including drinks, caviar, and some excursions.
- Service is personalized and responsive to individual preferences. Many have butler service as standard for all cabins.
- Open-seating dining is standard, meaning you do not have a set dining time each evening.
- There is less rigidity in enforcing rules such as the hours you can use the pool and hot tubs.

Cons:

- Fares are higher than those for similar itineraries run by mid-sized ships.
- Small cruise ships are not for those who want to remain anonymous, as crew and passengers will get to know you quickly.
- There will be fewer choices, although most of these ships have two or three dining room options, and will have some evening entertainment, a small casino, a spa, and a fitness center.
- They are not as welcoming of children, and are unlikely to offer kids' clubs other than during peak school holiday periods.

Many ships use decor designed to evoke the glory days of ocean liners. This is a grand staircase on the *MSC Preziosa*.

The Main Ocean Passenger Cruise Lines

The ten largest passenger cruise lines operating large and medium-sized ships, are:

- **Carnival**
  The world's largest cruise line offers fun, and good value for money. It promotes itself as providing 'Fun Ships', with constant entertainment and activities on deck, and throughout the ship. It also has child-friendly facilities and clubs.
- **Royal Caribbean**
  The world's second-largest cruise line offers a resort-like destination for cruisers, and constantly introduces features not seen on other ships, including rock climbing, surfing, ice skating, zip lining, and big production shows. It operates many of the largest cruise ships in the world. Royal Caribbean tries to attract all age ranges to fill the large ships, although it appeals especially to families.
- **Norwegian Cruise Lines**
  This company pioneered an informal approach to cruise travel, called 'Freestyle Cruising'. The overall ambiance is 'resort casual' and its flexible offering includes 20 different dining venues on board. The ships cater to a wide range of travelers including families, solo travelers, and couples.
- **MSC Cruises**
  The youngest of the major passenger cruise lines. Mediterranean based, it promises a 'Mediterranean Inspired Way of Life' on board, with a strong focus on family and food. It is a multilingual and multicultural ship, with six official languages spoken by staff, so it attracts cruisers from many countries.
- **Costa Cruises**
  A large European-based line with 60 years experience, promising 'Cruising Italian Style' in terms of ambience and food.
- **Princess Cruises**
  Well known in North America because one of the ships, the *Pacific Princess*, appeared in the television series *The Love Boat*. It was one of the pioneers in developing Alaskan cruises, and is one of the main players in the region,

owning lodges and tour companies as well as cruising in the region. Popular with couples and families.

- **Celebrity Cruises**
  Celebrity is a premium line promising 'modern luxury' for travelers. The decor and dining options on its ships are reminiscent of staying in a five-star hotel. It sails in all regions of the world, including the Galapagos and Hawaii.
- **Holland America**
  A century-old, luxury line, its Dutch heritage is reflected in the design, artwork, and artifacts. It has a high crew-to-passenger ratio, staterooms larger than many ships of similar size, and a focus on fine dining. It was the other pioneer in developing Alaskan cruising, and is a major operator in the region.
- **AIDA**
  Caters to the German market, and the main language on board is German. It is a relaxed and informal line with casual dress, self-service restaurants, and open seating. It has a big focus on fitness and health activities.
- **Disney Cruise Line**
  It is focused on families, with Disney-themed entertainment and decor, although it does provide adult-only areas and dining.

There are a few other large and medium-sized passenger cruise lines of significance:

- **Cunard Cruise Line**
  An icon of the cruise industry, sailing some of the most famous ships in the world: *Queen Mary 2, Queen Victoria and Queen Elizabeth*. It is best known for its British style, evoking the golden age of cruising, scheduled transatlantic crossings, and world cruises. It is the most formal of all the cruise lines in setting and enforcing a dress code on board, with a high proportion of formal nights on most cruises.
- **P&O Cruises**
  This major cruise line operating out of the UK is also owned by Carnival. It sails a selection of adult-only ships, small cruise ships, and large resort-style ships targeting families.

There are two leading small and boutique cruise ship lines:

- **Silversea**
  An ultra-luxury cruise line owned by the Lefebvre family of Rome, with Italian influence and style. It is an all-inclusive, all-suite line with many partnerships with luxury brands. Popular with professional couples and honeymooners, it also has explorer ships visiting the Galapagos, the Arctic, and Antarctica.
- **Seabourn Cruise Line**
  Owned by Carnival, it is also an ultra-luxury and all-inclusive line. The focus is on providing personalized service, including butler service in all suites.

Passengers take a walk on the deck of *Queen Mary 2* during a winter crossing from Southampton to New York.

The Memories

John Honeywell runs the cruise section for The Mirror newspaper, and is one of the best-known writers about cruising in the UK. He blogs at CaptainGreyBeard.com.

I have watched as blocks of ice as big as a house crashed into the sea from glaciers in Alaska, and I have held my sides with laughter as the Blue Man Group kept 700 passengers in thrall. I've taken excursions on rickety trains and swish catamarans in the Caribbean, and tasted wine and the most delicious tomatoes at a vineyard on the slopes of Mount Vesuvius, Italy.

I have gasped as Olympic-standard high divers plunged into a tiny pool on board the world's biggest cruise ship, and I have marveled from the wheelhouse of a converted fishing trawler as sea eagles soared over Scottish lochs. My mind has boggled at close-up magic tricks, and I have been kept on the edge of my seat by acrobatic feats my aching joints could not even contemplate.

The most memorable sunset of my life was at the glistening gold Shwedagon Pagoda in Yangon, Myanmar; it might have been matched by the early-morning sight of a polar bear in Spitsbergen, Norway, except that was in the land of the midnight sun, so there had been no dawn.

All these and many, many more magic moments I have been privileged to enjoy while cruising. And I have been fortunate to share the experiences with some wonderful people, old friends and new.

Adventure and Explorer Cruise Ships

Adventure and explorer ships carry between 50 and 200 passengers to more remote destinations. They are specially equipped to navigate the region they are serving. People using these ships are more interested in the destination than the ship and its amenities. The ships and their on-board environments reflect this attitude.

Pros:

- You will have access to places that are hard to reach any other way, such as the Hebridean Islands, Galapagos Islands, Falklands, Antarctica, Arctic, Iceland, Greenland, South Pacific Islands, and Norwegian coastline.
- It's a chance to focus on wildlife, nature viewing, and educational programs.
- You will be part of small groups that share a passion for adventure and nature travel.
- Passengers often have fascinating life experiences, adventures, and stories, and can make for engaging travel partners.

Cons:

- The quality of accommodation and range of facilities is less predictable, as this group of ships is less harmonious in design and usually owned by independent operators with differing standards.
- There will be a greater risk of encountering rough seas and seasickness. These ships are smaller, and do not have technology such as the stabilizers used by large cruise ships to reduce motion.
- Many of the routes head into or pass through some of the roughest stretches of sea to reach remote destinations, such as Drake's Passage on the way to Antarctica, the Gulf of Alaska, and the Cape of Good Hope at the base of Africa.

Main Explorer and Adventure cruise lines

Your choice of cruise lines will be dependent on the region you want to explore.

Explorer ships fall into four main categories.

1. **Regional experts:**

   You will usually be able to find independent providers who focus on and have expertise in a specific region, such as:

   - Hebridean Island Cruises (Scottish Islands);
   - *RMS Saint Helena* (Saint Helena and Ascension Islands); and
   - Quark Expeditions (Polar expeditions).

2. **Traditional maritime companies with a heritage of explorer cruising in a region, such as:**

   - Hapag-Lloyd, which has explorer ships operating in remote areas of the world including Antarctica, Asia, and the Amazon; and
   - Hurtigruten, which has been transporting goods and people up and down the Norwegian coastline for decades, and now also runs expeditions into the Arctic.

3. **Adventure travel companies expanding land-based adventure expertise into cruising, such as:**

   - National Geographic Magazine, which has a partnership with Lindblad Expeditions;
   - G Adventures, which runs the *MS Expedition* explorer ship; and
   - Noble Caledonian, which now operates cruise-explorer tours in the Arctic, Antarctica, and the South Pacific.

4. **Mainstream cruise lines expanding into explorer cruising in popular regions:**

   - Silversea Cruises now offers Galapagos cruises with the 100-passenger *Silver Galapagos* explorer ship, and sails to the Arctic and Antarctica with the 132-passenger *Silver Explorer* ship.

Tall Ship Sailing

Carrying between 20 and 200 passengers, tall ship sailing attracts romantics who are drawn to the idea of cruising under the power of billowing sails. They sail in island regions such as the Caribbean, Aegean Sea, and French Polynesia, where ports are close to each other. The reason for this is that they cruise slowly and want to minimize days at sea and offer as many stops as possible.

Pros:

- You will have a more traditional experience of being at sea; there is the ceremony of raising and unfurling the sails, often allowing the passengers to get involved in the process.
- You will feel you have stepped back in time. Sailing ships are built using traditional maritime materials and decor, with teak decks, brass fittings, and maritime-themed art.
- Many sailing ships have luxurious accommodation and facilities, including small casinos, spas, and fitness centers.
- Less formal than passenger cruise ships, guests on sailing ships are drawn together through the shared sense of adventure, and by informal activities on board.
- These ships offer pampering and comfort without requiring passengers to dress up. The clothing and style is smart casual.

Cons:

- The design of sailing ships is based on optimal use of space, making the layout more erratic and unusual. The corridors are narrow, with many stairs and no elevators, which make them unsuitable for people with mobility issues and physical disabilities.
- If you are expecting to be powered by wind all the time, you may be disappointed. They may operate on power more than half the time.
- Sailing boats move with the sea and wind, and are not suited to people prone to seasickness.
- Entertainment focuses on passenger participation activities, such as quizzes and games out on deck.

Main Tall Ship Sailing Cruise Lines

Three cruise lines lead tall ship sailing ship cruising.

1.Windstar:

It has a 'country club' style offering a smart/casual and refined experience.

2. **Star Clippers:**
   More informal, it operates three sailing ships and encourages passengers to get involved by participating in raising the sails or even having a go at the helm.
3. **Island Windjammers:**
   The more boisterous and party-style option, it is much more casual than the others. Dress code is t-shirts, swimsuits, and shorts.

Passengers coming off the *Star Flyer* tall ship in Saint Maarten.

Freighters

Many large container freight companies take fare-paying passengers on their ships. They usually carry fewer than 12 passengers, as maritime law requires them to carry a doctor on board if there is more than this number. Passengers are likely to be retirees or people on sabbaticals from work, as the shortest trips are around 30 days and the longest more than 100 days. Freighters are ideal for people with time on their hands, who love being at sea, and are looking for peace and quiet.

Pros:

- It is cheaper per day to take a freighter cruise than most other forms of cruising. Your only on-board costs will be drinks, and basics such as soap or laundry detergent, which you can buy from the on-board shop.
- You will have plenty of time to relax, unwind, and catch up on reading and hobbies. There will be many days at sea with no organized activities.
- There is no need to dress up for meals or events.
- The cabins will be equivalent to the officers' accommodation, with windows or portholes, private bathrooms, and air conditioning. Your cabin will be cleaned and bedding changed at least once a week.
- You will get three good meals a day, with the main meal usually being lunch. You eat with the crew, including the Captain and officers.
- Most passengers will be retired professionals, academics, and naval people with a passion for the sea.
- Freighters travel all around the world all the time.

Cons:

- You need to be able to travel for at least 30 days at a stretch.
- Passengers must be in good health, fit enough to manage all the stairs, and able to walk the long distances to get around the ship. Passengers have to submit a signed medical certificate from a doctor to this effect. Freighter companies restrict travel to adults under the age of 70.
- Schedule and ports can change based on changes in cargo bookings. You should not book a trip based on ensuring you get to specific ports at specific times.

- Most of the time is spent at sea, and stays in port may be limited to a few hours, as the Captain's aim is to load and offload cargo as quickly as possible and get back to sea.
- Freighters dock in commercial container ports away from the main city areas. As they are not accustomed to catering for passengers, it may not be easy to find nearby transportation to take you into town.
- Freighters do not have stabilizers, so there is a greater risk of seasickness.
- You are unlikely to have Internet access or mobile phone connections at sea, although the ship will have satellite phone contact for emergencies. Some ships may have satellite television, but most do not. Staying in touch with world events and news via shortwave radio can be unpredictable.

Main Freighter Lines

As the freighter ship experience is similar, cruisers looking to travel by freighter usually decide on the route they want to travel and the length of time, and then choose the line – so agents are key. The main agents for finding a passage on a freighter ship are Maris Freighter Cruise and Travel Club (freightercruises.com) and Maritime Cruises (maritime-cruises.com).

An excursion on a Rigid Inflatable Boat (RIB) passes Royal Caribbean's *Brilliance of the Seas* in the Norwegian Fjords.

The Igniting of a Passion

Danielle Fear blogs at CruiseMiss.com

I started cruising at 21 – and not by choice, I may add.

I was dragged kicking and screaming onto a 12-night Canary Islands voyage, and I was far from impressed. I had the stereotypical opinion that everyone on board would be tucked into bed by nine o'clock. My experience, however, was just the opposite, and rarely did I see my bed until long past two o'clock every morning. I packed so much into those 12 nights that I left feeling exhausted yet utterly liberated, and I couldn't wait to do it all again.

I am not your typical cruiser, and I like to think I cruise 'outside the box'. While other passengers get ready for an evening of entertainment in one of the on-board lounges, I prepare to enjoy some peace and simple things such as watching the sunset. I don't cruise to be kept entertained. I would say I don't even cruise for the food – however that would be a lie. What I do cruise for is to see the world, to meet people with the same passion, and to simply enjoy being free with nothing around for miles but deep blue sea.

Yachts

While the cost of private yacht charter is out of the reach of most travelers, you can cruise on yachts offering scheduled itineraries at fares similar to other cruising options. These are found in regions with ports in close proximity to each other, such as the islands in Greece, the Caribbean, the Maldives, and parts of Southeast Asia. They also operate in regions with major natural attractions, such as the Great Barrier Reef, the Galapagos, Alaska, and the Norwegian Fjords and coastline.

Pros

- It is a smaller and more intimate cruising option, carrying 100 passengers or less.
- It offers slow and less intense itineraries around one region, with many scenic stops and opportunities to engage in off-yacht activities in the water or on land.
- Sailing close to shore and in calmer waters, such as fjords, means you are likely to have calm seas.

Cons

- The cabins and public spaces are smaller.
- The facilities are limited. There will likely be only a lounge and dining area.
- You will find limited organized entertainment and on-board activities.
- Space on board to explore and find quiet corners to hide away and relax will be limited.
- Your enjoyment is reliant on the other passengers, and how well you get on with them.

Main Yacht Lines

As most yachts are run by small independent operators, and are destination focused, your choice will be driven first by your desired destination. The two main yacht cruise lines operating global schedules are SeaDream Yacht Club, which runs large yachts that are more like small ships and sails the Mediterranean and the Caribbean, and Variety Cruises, which focuses on Greece, the Indian Ocean, and Central America.

Monaco harbor is always packed full of luxury yachts.

River Cruise Ships

River cruising is a fast-growing segment of the cruise industry. These leisurely tours wind their way down rivers in Europe, Russia, China, Egypt, Vietnam, and the Mississippi in the United States. River cruises appeal to people who like escorted and packaged vacations, where everything has been taken care of. They tend to appeal and cater to passengers in their 50s, 60s and 70s.

Pros:

- Fares tend to be more inclusive than ocean passenger ships, and may include flights or fly-cruise packages, transfers to and from the ship, meals, drinks, and escorted excursions.
- River cruises often waive the single supplement, or reduce it for solo travelers.
- Accommodation will be good quality and comfortable, and all will have windows or balconies. The rooms are compact, due to the limitations on width and height to enable the ships to pass under bridges and through locks.
- You will receive a high level of service and attention. Ships are limited in size, carrying around 150 passengers, which enables the crew to get to know passengers and their needs.
- There will be constant scenery on both sides of the ship.
- Stops along the route will be frequent. Ships dock in the center of towns, allowing easy access for tours and exploring on your own.
- There will be a very low chance of seasickness.

Cons

- Independent travelers may find the pace too sedate. The routes, on-board facilities, entertainment and excursions are geared for a more mature audience.
- Entertainment options are limited, especially in the evenings. There are no theaters or casinos, and on-board entertainment will be limited.
- Trips can be disrupted by the state of rivers. In times of drought, ships struggle to reach some areas and, at other times, flooding causes severe disruption.

River Cruise Lines

Although many river cruise lines are focused on one region, the main European companies have now expanded into Asia.

The main river cruising lines in Europe and Asia are:

- **Viking River Cruises**
  The world's largest river cruise line. Operates on the main rivers in Europe, including the Rhine, Danube, Elba, Douro, Rhone, and Seine. It also operates in Russia and on the Yangtze River in China. It offers Scandinavian design and service.
- **Uniworld**
  Operates cruises in Europe, Russia, China, Vietnam, Cambodia, and Egypt. A luxury river cruise line promising a boutique hotel experience.
- **AmaWaterways**
  Operates in Europe, Russia, Vietnam, Cambodia, and Botswana. It is also a luxury line, with a strong focus on food.

River cruising in the United States:
River cruising is focused on the Mississippi River, with the American Queen Steamboat Company and American Cruise Lines being the main operators.

Canal Barges

Many European countries, including France, the United Kingdom, Ireland, Belgium, Italy, Holland, and Portugal, have thousands of miles of canals crossing the countryside. These were used to transport goods before being replaced by motorways, railways, and air travel. The canals are now peaceful waterways offering small self-drive charters and luxury hotel barges. Barge travel is suited to travelers who are less concerned about seeing major tourist attractions, and want to explore out-of-the-way destinations.

Pros:

- You will travel at a leisurely pace, winding through the countryside. Barges cover short distances each day, and the locks slow down the process, allowing for a lot of off-barge activities.

Barge Charter Pros:

- Very limited instruction is required before you are able to navigate through the canals and locks.
- They are suitable for families and groups of friends traveling together, as you can stop whenever you want, allowing people to leave the barge to go walking or hiking and rejoin further down the canal.

Hotel Barges Pros:

- These are small and intimate, carrying up to 20 guests.
- Fares include your accommodation, food, drinks, excursions, transport to places that are not in walking distance, and bicycles.
- Hotel barges have plush sitting rooms and dining rooms, and comfortable cabins. Most will also have air conditioning and Internet access.
- Operators take great pride in the food and wine from the regions they tour, and place a lot of emphasis on serving gourmet meals.
- Informal and casual clothing is the norm.

Cons

- Barges are small with limited space. However, if you feel trapped you can easily step off and walk alongside the barge on the banks if you want to stretch your legs.
- Cabins are compact with limited space for luggage.
- There are few facilities such as laundry, TV, and entertainment and no medical amenities.
- Barges are not suitable for people with limited mobility or physical disabilities.

Main Canal Cruising Lines

The best way to charter a barge or find a hotel barge is through an agent such as The Barge Company (bargecompany.com). There are also some companies that own a number of barges in different countries. The leader in this is European Waterways (gobarging.com), which owns and operates hotel barges in the UK, Ireland, France, Germany, Holland, and Italy.

Permanent Residential Ships

The main residential ship providing permanent accommodation is The World.

It was launched in 2002, and constantly travels around the world. Many owners rent out their apartments to travelers who are looking for longer trips, and want to cruise in an upmarket self-catering resort rather than a full service cruise ship. There are restaurants, a spa, a fitness center and a pool on the ship.

Educational Ships

There are a number of ongoing educational cruises with regular schedules:

- Semester at Sea. It provides undergraduate courses on a dedicated cruise ship. Run in partnership with the University of Virginia, it offers courses on anthropology, theater, history, and politics, combining lectures with experiences in the ports of call. A course of 100 days visits 15 countries and has 15 to 20 ports of call.
- University at Sea. Providing continuing education courses for the medical profession, this organization takes space on scheduled cruises on mainstream passenger cruise lines. They run lectures on sea days, allowing course members to travel with their friends and family and tour with them on port days.

Permanently Docked Cruise Ships

There are a number of retired cruise liners that operate as moored hotels and tourist attractions.

There are three main cruise ships you can tour and stay in:

1. The *Queen Mary* is in Long Beach, California. This art-deco styled ship has been docked here since retiring in 1967.
2. The *SS Rotterdam* in Rotterdam, Holland. This ship was the pride of the Dutch in the heyday of transatlantic crossings. You can stay in cabins decorated in a 1950s style.
3. The *Queen Elizabeth 2*. It sailed for 40 years on world cruises and transatlantic crossings before being retired in 2008. It is being converted into a luxury hotel and residences, and will be located at a port in Asia.

The original SS Rotterdam ocean liner is now a hotel moored in Rotterdam.

Through The Lines

Mike Faust blogs at CruiseCurrents.com

I've been cruising for almost my entire life. All 17 years of it.

I have been on more than 12 cruises, and as I grow up, my interests and cruising activities keep changing. As a young boy cruiser on Disney, I enjoyed hanging out in the kid's club making slime, and exploring the ship on organized scavenger hunts. I then wanted to make a transition out of the kid's clubs to explore on my own, and I became more fascinated by the ship itself. I was increasingly intrigued by the intricate workings of cruise ships, and loved the behind-the-scenes tours.

This led to me wanting to travel on cruise lines with long maritime traditions and traditional cruise experiences such as the historic Holland America Line. Now, as a 17-year-old, I am thrilled by the classic experience and design of long-established cruise lines with wrap-around promenades and traditional maritime decor.

Many teens nowadays prefer cruise lines that offer distractions such as water slides and kid's clubs. But for me, the experience of cruising, and the art of sailing across the seas on ships that hark back to the traditions of cruising, is a perfect voyage.

I love that cruising has so many choices. As my tastes change, I will be able to find new and different lines to match my changing interests.

Main Cruising Destinations

The main cruising regions are the Caribbean and the Mediterranean, but new ones are emerging as travelers demand greater adventures and ever more places to see. These are the main destination options currently available.

Ocean Cruising Destinations

Taster cruises

A taster cruise offers an inexpensive way to determine if cruising, or a cruise line, is for you. They last two to four nights, and are good value as they venture to destinations close to the embarkation port. Although they are increasingly used as party trips by people looking for low-cost breaks with lots of food and cheap drink, they are still ideal for helping you decide if cruising suits you, and to banish any fears of getting seasick.

Caribbean

The Caribbean is the most popular cruise region in the world, with most cruises sailing out of the Florida ports of Miami, Fort Lauderdale, and Port Canaveral between October and April to avoid the hurricane season. These cruises visit islands that are close to Florida to reduce days at sea and maximize port calls. East Caribbean itineraries visit islands such as Saint Maarten, Saint Thomas, and Antigua. Western itineraries go to places such as Cozumel, Grand Cayman, and Jamaica.

In addition to the US-based cruise lines such as Carnival and Royal Caribbean sailing out of Florida, European cruise lines move their ships to the region during the European winter. Rather than sailing out of Florida, they usually start and end their itineraries on islands in the Caribbean, such as Barbados, and include more southerly islands on their itineraries.

There are some things you should consider if you plan to cruise in the Caribbean:

- The major ports in the region get very busy. The three popular cruise ports close to Florida are Puerto Rico, Saint Thomas, and Saint Maarten. They receive millions of cruise visitors annually, and can have as many as seven ships in port each day. I recommend going on a more southerly Caribbean itinerary that originates and returns to one of the islands. You will visit islands such as Barbados, Grenada, Dominica, and Saint Lucia that have a more authentic Caribbean feel than the more tourist-focused northern part of the region.
- Check all your ports of call before deciding on a cruise. A number of cruise lines own uninhabited islands they include as stops to provide a day of resort experiences.
- The islands can blur into a haze of sameness if you stick to doing only catamaran, zip lining, and beach excursions in every port. Take in excursions on the islands, and explore the history and uniqueness of each port of call.
- A Caribbean cruise is great for getting a taste of the different islands. You can then decide which to return to for a longer land-based vacation.

Mediterranean

The Mediterranean is the next most popular cruise region, providing a mix of sun and different European cultures as the ships call on multiple countries. The season runs from April to October, and most of the cruises originate out of Barcelona, Venice, Genoa, and Southampton.

Here are some considerations if you plan to cruise in the Mediterranean:

- Check the ports on your itinerary to see how many are docking in the actual city. Ports billed as calling on cities such as Rome, Florence, and Paris have to dock in ports that are hours away from the city. Look for ports that say things such as 'Rome (from Civitavecchia)' or 'Livorno (Florence/Pisa)'. If you want to visit these cities, check how far the journey is from the port.
- Sail from ports in the Mediterranean such as Barcelona, Genoa, or Venice, rather than ports such as Southampton or Hamburg that require additional sea days to get into the region.
- Consider lines using smaller ships and yachts, as they can call into more unusual and smaller ports in the region.

Alaska

Most cruises are seven days long, and focus on one of two routes:

- The Inside Passage is a web of waterways between islands, created centuries ago by glaciers. They offer incredible scenery and wildlife. These cruises are usually round trips from Vancouver or Seattle.
- The Gulf of Alaska is further north, where you can see the largest glaciers in the country. These cruises are one-way to Anchorage from either Vancouver or Seattle.

There are a few things to take into consideration if you plan to cruise in Alaska:

- The weather is unpredictable, and often wet and chilly. The season runs from May to September, with June and July likely to be the best. Popular excursions such as flying over the glaciers may be cancelled due to weather.
- The sea in the Gulf of Alaska is known for being rough and turbulent.
- In addition to the mainstream passenger cruise lines, consider explorer cruises that use smaller ships and visit more out-of-the-way places.

Norwegian Fjords

The Norwegian Fjords were carved out of the hard rock by massive glaciers of ice. They go as far as 130 miles inland from the sea, can be 1,300 yards deep, and are wide enough for passenger cruise ships to sail right into them. The season is the same as in Alaska, with the peak time being July and August.

If you plan to cruise the Norwegian Fjords there are some things you should think about:

- Ensure the itinerary includes a high proportion of villages in the Fjords, and not too many large towns, such as Bergen and Stavanger. The villages give you a real sense of the region.
- Sailing from ports in Europe, such as Southampton, will give you only two or three of the seven days in the Fjords. Sail from ports within the region to ensure that you see more of the Fjords in the same amount of time. Consider explorer cruise lines that use smaller ships calling on many towns along the coast and in the Fjords.

Baltics

A cruise in the Baltic Sea takes you to Sweden, Estonia, Finland, and Saint Petersburg in Russia. Most spend two or three full days in Saint Petersburg to allow time to explore the city's rich treasures in the various museums.

There are some considerations if you plan to cruise the Baltics:

- You can go on cruise line and private tours without having a Russian visa. If you want to self-tour, you will need a visa. It is a fairly complex procedure, as you will need to acquire an invitation letter (which the cruise line can arrange) and visit the Russian Embassy to process the application.
- The attractions in Saint Petersburg, such as the Hermitage and Saint Catherine's Palace, get very crowded, so book early morning excursions. Some cruise lines have tours that get you into attractions before the official opening time.

Transatlantic Cruises

There are two ways to cross the Atlantic.

- The Classic Crossing: Cunard *Queen Mary 2* is the only ship offering regular scheduled crossings. They last seven or eight days with no ports of call.
- Repositioning Crossings: Ships are moved between Europe and the Caribbean and South America at the start and end of the cruising seasons. These cruises last ten to 14 days, with one week touring one of the regions and one week crossing the Atlantic.

World Cruises

Most passenger cruise lines offer a cruise that circumnavigates the world between January and April each year. Traveling by freighter at any time of the year is another option. Both options last for at least 100 days but you can also book segments of the trip.

Emerging Cruise Destinations

The following are growing in popularity and the number of cruising options available is increasing.

- **Arctic and Antarctica:** Traditionally the focus for niche explorer cruise lines, cruises in these regions are now also being offered by mainstream cruise lines.
- **Galapagos:** This region has to be explored by smaller explorer ships and yachts, although Silversea has been granted a license.
- **Australia, New Zealand, and Pacific:** A popular destination for world cruises, companies are now placing ships in the region to run cruises circumnavigating Australia and New Zealand, and exploring the Pacific Islands.
- **South and Central America:** Cruising is growing fast in South America, and many mainstream cruise companies run cruises touring around the continent. Passing through the Panama Canal in Central America is also a highlight on many world cruises, and on voyages traveling from the Caribbean up to Los Angeles or across to Hawaii. There are many independent ocean cruise providers in the region, which provide trips such as those along the Chilean Patagonian coast, and between Panama and Colombia.
- **Hawaii:** Growing in popularity, Hawaii is especially favored for special events and honeymoons. Options are limited, and most cruises are from the West Coast of America, and are two weeks long with many sea days.
- **Asia:** There are a number of Asia-based cruise companies. Most mainstream cruise lines offer voyages through the region as part of their world cruises.
- **Africa, the Middle East, and the Indian Ocean:** As with Asia, it is more usual to cruise the region as part of a longer voyage. However, some cruise lines have started to place ships in South Africa.

Freighter Cruising Destinations

You can travel to any of the main commercial regions of the world on a freighter. Freighter journeys fall into two main types.

1. Return trips to a specific region, such as from Europe to West Africa and back, China to Europe and back, or the United States to Europe and back. These last between 30 to 50 days; and
2. Circumnavigations of the world. You can either sail west from Europe to the United States, through the Panama Canal and back to Europe via Australia and Asia, or sail east from Europe through the Suez Canal, visiting many Asian ports before sailing down to Australia and back.

The port of Civitavecchia is called Rome on many cruises. It is two hours from the city!

The Vantage Point

Jane Chadwick blogs at gocruisewithjane.co.uk

When I'm on a cruise I often lean on the rails of the deck and recall what I have seen from that very same spot on previous cruises on the same ship.

From that vantage point, I have seen the sea look angry and attempt to jump up to the rail. But I have also seen the sea as flat as a blue millpond, with dolphins breaking the water. I've watched sunrises and sunsets, and I have seen the stars shine brighter than anywhere else.

That same spot on deck has shown me Saint Mark's Square in Venice, and the Sydney Opera House. I've watched the Statue of Liberty stand tall and proud as we approached Manhattan, and seen tiny remote villages and islands in the Fjords. And, as I've sailed toward Caribbean Islands, I've heard the sound of a distant reggae band.

One place I am always sad to see from that spot is my final disembarkation port, which never looks quite as attractive as the place we departed from at the start of the cruise.

River Cruising Destinations

River cruises are widely available in a number of areas:

- **Europe:** The most developed region in the world for river cruising is Europe. The Rhine and Danube Rivers in Central Europe, the Seine in France, the Po in Italy, and the Douro in Portugal are all popular.
- **Asia:** The main cruises in Asia are on the Yangtze River in China, taking travelers to Shanghai and Beijing, and the Mekong River in Vietnam and Cambodia.
- **Africa:**
  - **Egypt:** River cruising down the Nile from Luxor to the Valley of the Kings and Queens has been established for decades. The peak season is from October to May, when Egypt is slightly cooler, but you can travel year round. You can also take a traditional felucca sailing boat, but these are mostly used for day trips as accommodation is basic.
  - **Southern Africa:** The *Zambezi Queen* is a luxury river cruiser that operates on the Chobe River on the border of Botswana and Namibia.
- **Amazon, South America:** While cruise ships can go up the Amazon River in the Brazilian section, you need to take a river cruise or barge to get further up the Amazon. There are many independent river and barge cruise providers that can take you along the Amazon and the various rivers running off it, with accommodations ranging from the plush to the basic.
- **United States:** You can find river cruises around many parts of the country, including upstate New York and the rivers of Florida, but the most developed river cruising takes place on the Mississippi River.

A cycling tour is a popular way to explore destinations as you exercise while exploring.

Choosing the Right Cabin

While your budget is going to be key in determining which grade of cabin you can afford, there are a number of variables and considerations I recommend you take into account before selecting a specific cabin on your chosen ship. You may be able to spend less and still have a memorable vacation.

Types of Cabins

You will often find passengers and cruise lines refer to cabins as staterooms. Here are the four main grades of cabins from the most expensive to least:

1. **Suites:** These vary greatly in size and splendor based on the ship, starting with 'mini-suites', and increasing in size and facilities through 'suites', 'owner's suites', and finally, 'grand suites'. Suites often come with benefits such as a stocked and replenished mini-bar, and priority embarkation and disembarkation. On some cruise lines, the suites will have their own restaurant, lounge, pool and deck area, dedicated concierge, and butler service.
2. **Balcony cabins:** New-build cruise and river ships aim to have a majority of balcony cabins, as these are the most popular. They have a sleeping area, a small seating area with a table, a dressing table, and a balcony with two chairs and a small table.
3. **Exterior cabins with windows:** In modern ships, these are lower down in the ship and will have either large picture windows or portholes. In some older cruise ships, these are the majority of cabins as many were built when balconies were not in vogue. Explorer, adventure and freight ships have these cabins as the norm.
4. **Inside cabins:** These will be the least expensive option. They have no external facing windows, and are smaller than balcony cabins. They usually only have a bed, a dressing table and a shower room. Some cruise lines are introducing large TV panels that project an outside view to make the rooms feel less claustrophobic.

Make sure you do not spend more than you really need to

Even if your budget can stretch to one of the premium grades of cabin, consider the following before you make your decision. You may be able to spend less and still have an unforgettable experience.

The cruise itinerary

The time of year, destination, mix of port days and sea days and scenery should be taken into account when deciding which cabin is ideal for your trip. If the weather and scenery are going to be spectacular, having your own balcony will add a great deal to your enjoyment of the experience. If not, a less expensive window or inside cabin can be a better option as you can venture out on deck to enjoy entering or leaving port. For example, we booked a balcony cabin on a winter transatlantic crossing and, due to the cold and short days, never used it for more than a few minutes a day.

Your routine and degree of sociability

If you enjoy quiet time to yourself and do not like sitting out on deck or in public spaces, a larger cabin with a balcony or window will better suit your lifestyle. If you will only use your cabin to change and sleep for a few hours after a long night of partying, then you may only need a basic room such as an interior cabin, even if your budget can stretch to a higher grade.

Number of travelers in your party

Most cabins are designed for double occupancy. Most cruise lines charge extra for solo or additional person occupancy of cabins. If you are traveling as a family, with a third person, or as a solo traveler you can save money by using a cruise line and ship catering for your party size.

- Solo Travelers: *Norwegian Epic* has many solo cabins, as do most P&O Cruise line ships. Holland America and Swan Hellenic will frequently run solo traveler deals. River cruise lines are less likely to have solo occupancy surcharges.
- Family and Group Travel: Not surprisingly, the Disney Cruise Line has many options for families traveling together, including bunk beds for children and adjoining cabins. Most of the large resort-style cruise ships have more options for family suites and adjoining rooms.

Choosing the exact cabin within your chosen type

Most cruise lines will allow you to choose the specific cabin number once you have decided on the type of cabin. The following should be taken into account when making your selection:

Port or starboard cabins

Port is the left hand side of the ship as you face forward, and starboard is the right. Historically, ships had loading and unloading capability on the port side. Cruise and river ships can dock on either side, so port-side cabins do not guarantee you will be facing land when you dock.

Select a port or starboard cabin based on the scenery you may encounter. For example, sailing into New York you will pass the Statue of Liberty on the port side, and you will pass it on the starboard side when you depart. If you are sailing northward up the Norwegian Coast, a starboard cabin will have constant views of the stunning landscape, and port cabins will have it when sailing southward.

Distance to the entertainment, restaurants, and facilities

This is more important on passenger cruise ships than on river and explorer ships. The distance from one end of the ship to the other can be many hundreds of yards. If walking distances is an issue for you, use the deck plans available in the brochure or on the cruise line's website to help you choose a cabin closest to the areas of the ship you are likely to use most, such as the restaurant, swimming pool, or casino.

Fear of, or prone to, seasickness

If you have a fear of seasickness, the cabins with the least movement on a cruise ship will be low down and near to the center of the ship. This is where a ship pivots and moves least if it encounters rough seas.

Concern over noise

If you are concerned about noise, or like to sleep in late, avoid cabins that are:

- under restaurants, especially the self-service buffet where there will be a lot of movement and scraping of chairs as people come and go;

- under the promenade or open decks. You are likely to have the sound of joggers, walkers, or the deck furniture being set up and moved about; and
- above or below the disco or where exercise classes are being held, as loud music can seep through into the cabin.

Traditional English afternoon tea is served on many cruise ships.

Budgeting

When budgeting for your cruise, take into account what different cruise lines include or exclude in their fares. While cruise fares include 'full board' (accommodation, breakfast, lunch, and dinner), each line takes a different approach to what else will be included. Add-on items can make a significant difference to the total cost of your trip.

There are three areas to focus on when budgeting for your cruise.

Understand exactly what is included in the fare

You need to add into your budget everything that is not included in the fare. Specifically, check if the fare being offered to you includes the following:

- Flights and transfers to and from the ship.
- Drinks, including soft drinks, alcohol, and teas/coffees.
- Gratuities. These could add $5 to $20 per day, per person. There are three main approaches to gratuities:
  - Included in the fare. You are not expected by the crew or the cruise line to tip while on board.
  - Added to your on-board account at a rate determined by the cruise line.
  - Left to your discretion to give directly to the crew. The cruise line usually provides a suggested daily rate and envelopes to put it in.
- Excursions. These could add between $50 and $150 per person, per excursion.
- Free shuttle-bus transfers into town in all ports of call.

Budget for the additional costs you will incur before the cruise

Add in payments you will have to make before your cruise:

- Travel insurance. Good insurance is essential to cover cancellation, illness, and repatriation should you fall ill or need to return home.
- Visas and inoculations.
- Credit card charges. There may be a levy for using a credit card to pay for the cruise. You are not usually charged a fee for using a debit card.
- Costs of getting to and from the ship not included in your fare, including parking costs if leaving your car at the port.

- Additional baggage charges if you are flying to your port city.
- Overnight accommodation if staying at the port before or after the cruise.

Budget for the costs you will incur while on the cruise

The cruise line will be aiming to get you to spend as much they can while on board. You need to budget for and control your spending. The items you should include in your budget are as follows:

- **Gratuities:** Even if covered in your fare, you may want to tip for outstanding service and tour guides.
- **Drinks:** You may have to pay a surcharge for special cocktails, champagne, and premium brands. Cruise lines sell wine, cocktail, and soft-drink packages based on a per-day charge. If you drink alcohol, these packages may save you money and help control your on-board spend. Many cruise lines will not let you bring your own drinks on the ship, and they may search for and confiscate it. Check if your cruise line allows you to bring it on board before you waste money trying to bring it on your ship.
- **Specialty dining charges:** While your cruise fare will include meals in at least one venue, cruise lines have added specialty restaurants and charge a fee to dine there. Charges can range from a modest $5 to a more substantial $75 per person.
- **Photographs:** Every time you board or go to an event, and even at some meals, you will have your photograph taken. They can cost $10 or more each if you decide to purchase them.
- **Internet access:** Access to Wi-Fi will cost anywhere from $0.25 to $1 per minute. Most cruise lines will sell discounted packages of Internet access.
- **Telephone calls:** Including mobile phone roaming and usage charges.
- **Spa:** Treatments can cost from $80 and up per session.
- **Fitness classes:** Many of the larger cruise ships run Zumba, yoga, and exercise classes at an additional cost. This could cost around $50 for a seven-day cruise.
- **Gambling and gaming costs:** From casinos to bingo.
- **Laundry and dry cleaning:** Costs will be comparable to those on land. Most cruise lines offer free self-laundry and ironing rooms.
- **Shopping:** Including art auctions, jewelry, tax-free items and souvenirs.

Tips on minimizing your spend on board

I am often asked how you can counter the 'tricks' used by cruise lines to get you to spend more on board. While there are some steps you can take, by far the best solution is to set a daily budget, monitor it, and stick to it. There are some things that will help you to avoid overspending:

- Staying clear of all promotional activities. This includes merchandise sales tables, shopping talks, art shows and auctions, and on-board stores.
- Taking your own photographs while boarding and on formal nights.
- Not buying the special cocktails and champagne on offer at sail-away parties.
- Attending the Captain's cocktail parties and other events where there are free drinks and snacks.
- Buying the specially priced drinks packages.
- Drinking the complimentary juices, teas, and coffees at meals and in the buffet dining room, versus ordering around the pool or in the bars.
- Not using, or using very selectively, the specialty restaurants.
- Drinking the ship's water, versus buying bottled water.
- Not playing games such as bingo. Do not gamble in the casino or take part in the competitions run there.
- Doing your own laundry, versus sending it to the ship service.
- Checking email and accessing the Internet when you are in port and can find free Wi-Fi stations. Ask the crew or follow where they go, as they will know where the closest free ones are.
- Following my advice and tips on excursions later in the book.

Smaller cruise ships will often dock right in the city, such as in Bergen.

My Annual Family Reunion

Daniel Abrahams blogs at mytravelmoney.co.uk/articles

One of the most charming aspects of my youth was spending every Christmas on the *Queen Elizabeth 2*. While the decor of the ship was pretty 'old school' compared to more modern cruise liners, it had an atmosphere and community that we were drawn to year after year – and we were not the only ones. It was like attending a family reunion.

Each night before dinner, my whole family would sit in the lounge excitedly chattering away with other families we had grown to love over the years. There was Marvin the New York doctor, Mr. Cohen from Stanmore, and many other 'regulars' who made sure there was never a dull moment. They all watched me and my brothers grow from boys into teens, and become adults.

It was not only the passengers that we saw every year that made us feel like we were among family. I remember a time when I was around 12 years old and sharing a cabin with my parents. They were getting ready for a formal night while our lovely cabin crew, Colin and Mary, sat on one of the beds chatting to us for 20 minutes about our day. They became an extended part of the family. We looked forward to seeing them each year.

Although I truly believe there will never be anything like the magic of that now retired ship again, we still have our annual family reunions, despite having grown up and left home. The family meets on a ship every Christmas, and we still see many of the old friends we have made over the years – both crew and passengers.

6 Tips for Getting the Best Fare

You will obviously be looking to pay as little as possible for your cruise, while the cruise company is looking to extract as much as they can from you. Getting the best price for a cruise requires you to be active and involved in seeking, tracking, and negotiating to get the best deal.

In the previous section on budgeting, I showed the importance of understanding the total cost of your cruise, not just looking at the basic fare. When looking for the best cruise deals, it is important to make sure you factor in the hidden costs and add-ons.

I have six tips to ensure you get the best cruise fares.

1. The more flexible you are, the lower the fare
Flexibility is the key to getting low fares. If you are set on going on a specific cruise on a specific date, in a specific cabin, you are more likely to pay a premium to ensure you get exactly what you want. If you are completely flexible on where you go, when you go, and what grade or cabin you travel in, you can get a better fare as you can book late when prices are set at levels to fill empty cabins.

Most travelers will fall between these two extremes, so when looking at how flexible you are prepared to be, consider the following:

- River cruises often get booked up more quickly than ocean cruises. This will change as capacity is growing.
- There is more competition in the main cruise destinations such as the Caribbean and the Mediterranean, so the chances of finding better deals are greater.
- The start and end of the cruising season in a region will offer greater flexibility as it is less popular and the weather is less predictable. April/May and September/October in the Caribbean and Mediterranean or winter transatlantic crossings are good bets.

- Economic strength in a region affects demand. The economic pressures in Europe, and the high cost of flying there from North America due to increased fuel costs, has weakened demand and reduced fares.
- Avoid new ship launches and maiden seasons as these tend to be in demand and more expensive. Instead, consider cruising on other ships in that cruise line's fleet, as there are often deals because most passengers want to travel on the new ship.

2. Sign up for the cruise line emails/mailings for promotional offers

This is the best way to keep informed about promotional fares. Most cruise lines have active direct marketing activities and send out regular updates with new offers.

Here are the types of special offer fares favored by cruise lines:

- **On-board credits:** Cruise lines often run promotions offering OBC (on-board credit). This is a credit to your on-board account that offsets the cost of excursions, drinks, spa services, gratuities, shop purchases made on ship, and entertainment activities.
- **Balcony and level upgrades:** In this case, you might book a cabin with a window, but will be guaranteed an upgrade to a cabin with a balcony.
- **Non-refundable saver fares:** These are restricted fares that do not usually allow you to choose a specific cabin, only the grade. Like non-refundable airline fares, you have to pay the full fare at the time of booking, and the cancellation charges will be 100 percent of the fare. They are often available five or six months before a cruise.
- **Late offers:** These are, as you would expect, for cruises that are departing soon after the booking date. They tend to be departures within the following 90-day period. Travelers have to pay the final balance on any existing bookings three months before departure, so the cruise line has a good understanding of how full the ship will be. You usually have to pay in full at time of booking for these offers.
- **Military discounts:** Many cruise lines offer special fares and promotions on cruises to serving and retired military personnel. The best offers and availability are for United States and Canadian military on cruises out of North American ports.

3. Book a guaranteed grade of cabin, versus a specific cabin

Instead of booking a specific cabin, just book within your desired grade.

Close to departure you will be allocated a cabin. It is possible you will be allocated a superior cabin to those who paid to be in a specific one. By giving the cruise line the flexibility to allocate your cabin around those preferring to pay a premium for a specific one, you may receive an unexpected bonus. For example, we once found ourselves in a huge penthouse with two bathrooms, a dining area, a lounge, and a bedroom despite paying the lowest fare in the grade. On the other hand, we once found ourselves in a restricted mobility room in the same grade.

4. Use a cruise agent to negotiate and book your cruise

Cruise lines have advanced online booking systems that allow you to book a cruise, select a cabin, and book add-ons like pre- and post-cruise hotels, flights, parking, excursions, transfers, or parking. However, when it comes to cruising, it is better to work with an expert cruise agent. In my experience, you are more likely to get a better deal or get more extras included.

5. Book your next cruise on board

If there is a cruise booking office on your ship, book your next cruise while you are still on board. You will receive extra offers, such as on-board credits or upgrades.

You should be able to have the booking attributed to your agent, so they will still get their commission and you can keep a strong relationship with them.

6. Once booked, keep checking the price

The price of your cruise will fluctuate. Keep an eye on the prices and promotions offered. There are online sites that will track fare movements and alert you of changes. Some charge a small fee for the service, but they may save you significant amounts of money. They are listed in the resources section of this book. If you see a reduction, immediately contact your cruise agent or cruise line if you booked directly with them. The cruise line will match, in some way, the discount fare. I have been able to get upgrades and additional on-board credits by tracking fares after I had booked.

A small-boat tour around Dominica took us to remote fishing villages.

Cruise Contracts Advice

When you pay the fare for your cruise, you are accepting the terms of the cruise line contract. Make sure you understand what you are agreeing to before you book. I have seen many complaints on cruise discussion boards from passengers about the compensation they received when things went wrong. Unfortunately, it is often what they agreed to in their contract. The cruise lines do often provide more compensation than the contract requires for public relations purposes and to retain clients, but it is best to know what you are signing up for.

To address the concerns about compensation in the industry, the members of the Cruise Lines International Association (CLIA) launched a Passenger Bill of Rights in 2013[4], capturing many of the existing good practices for dealing with passengers when things go wrong on a cruise. Ask if your cruise line subscribes to the bill, and how many of the terms have been built into the contract. Visit the official CLIA site (cruising.org) to find out more about the content of the bill.

You should understand what will happen in the following situations.

Personal Events

By understanding what the cruise contract provides for, you can take out additional insurance to supplement areas where you feel exposed. Here are the main things to look for:

- What if you want to change the date or cancel your cruise? Your contract may count any change as a cancellation and you could lose your entire deposit or fare.
- What if there is an illness or death in the family that prevents you from traveling? Make sure you are clear about how 'family member' is defined in the contract.
- What if you want to substitute one member of your party for someone else? A change in name may be taken as a cancellation.
- What if you or a member of your party falls ill during the cruise and has to leave the ship? You should also understand what arrangements would be made for family members if someone dies on board.

Cruise Line Events

- What if your cruise is cancelled before departure? Check what refunds and compensation will be offered, including for items linked to the cruise that you booked through the line or by yourself (airfares, excursions, etc).
- What if your cruise is abandoned part way through due to technical issues?
- What if the advertised itinerary is changed before you cruise, and ports of call are dropped or altered?

Additional Considerations

- What country's law will apply in the case of any legal dispute or incident, such as theft or personal injury? Most cruise ships are registered in 'ports of convenience', such as Panama, the Bahamas, and Liberia. This means the law of those countries applies, irrespective of where the cruise line head office is or where you bought your ticket. The law in ports of convenience can be more favorable for the cruise line.
- What rights are you agreeing to waive? These could include permitting the cruise line to take photos of you and use them in their promotional materials, limits on your ability to use images and photos that you have taken, and allowing staff to search you, your bags, and your cabin whenever they wish.

Chocolate buffets are a popular treat on many cruises.

Packing Advice and Tips

How much luggage should you take?

Ocean cruise ships do not limit how much luggage you can take, nor do they require you to handle your bags from the time you arrive at the port to the time you leave. Your bags will be taken by porters, delivered to your cabin and removed from outside your cabin, and taken to the dockside at the end of the cruise.

Freighter ships allow you to bring as much luggage as you can carry yourself. All other cruise ships usually restrict luggage to one large suitcase and one carry-on bag due to limited space on board.

If you are planning to self-disembark at the end of the cruise, only take luggage you can carry off the ship without assistance. Self-disembarking is the earliest way to depart from a ship once it has been cleared by the port authorities. It allows you to avoid waiting for your allocated time slot, which can be many hours later.

Clothing to consider

If there is a dress code and a number of special events, you may require clothes for 'formal evenings', which means long, formal gowns for women and black tie for men. Then there are 'semi-formal evenings', which generally means cocktail dresses for women and jackets with or without ties for men, and 'smart casual evenings', which means smart dresses or trousers for women, and long-sleeved or smart shirts and slacks for men. Each line has different codes and degrees to which they enforce them, so make sure you have checked and come prepared.

If you anticipate a range of weather or the nature of the cruise is adventure, pack clothes that can be layered for multiple situations.

Carry-on luggage

Assume that your bags will be delivered to your cabin only once your ship departs, and use this list as a guide to what to put in your carry-on bag:

- Passport.
- Alternative photo ID, such as a driver's license.
- Cruise tickets.
- Credit card, or sufficient cash to cover on-board spend. You have to provide a credit card when you check in to guarantee your on-board spend. If you do not want to use a credit card, you can deposit cash instead. Some cruise lines do not take debit cards, so check in advance.
- Valuables including cameras, laptops, credit cards, and cash.
- Travel insurance documents and emergency contact numbers.
- Copies of visas and inoculation certificates.
- Items you are likely to need before your bags arrive in your cabin, e.g. something warm in case it is cold on deck, or swimwear if you want to swim or use the hot tub before the ship departs.
- Prescription medication.

Non-clothes items to pack

In addition to clothing, here are some items to add to your list:

- Plug adaptors. Cruise ships usually have American-style electric plugs, and 110-120 volts. Some also have European plug sockets. Having a couple of universal adaptors in your luggage can be helpful.
- Cables and chargers for all your electronic items.
- Earplugs and eyeshades may be helpful.
- First aid kit. Bring remedies for ailments such as seasickness, headaches and diarrhea, along with bandages. The medical center is expensive to use and the on-board shops, which are only open out of port, will not sell over-the-counter medicines.
- Sunscreen.
- Travel alarm clock.
- Highlighter pen. To mark up and plan your day in the daily program.
- Guide books and maps if you are planning to self-tour in some ports.
- Entertainment (e.g. iPod, iPad, eBook reader, or books).
- Small backpack to use when on excursions, to carry your camera, identification, water, and something warm, if needed.

- Two-way radios are helpful for families and groups traveling together to stay in touch and make arrangements, because mobile phone usage is expensive, and sometimes impossible.
- Scan copies of important documents such as your passport, insurance documents, and visas, and email them to yourself, or make photocopies and leave them with a family member or friend. Should you lose any of them, you will be able to access full copies of all these key documents.

Some cruise lines require black tie and formal gowns on 'formal evenings'.

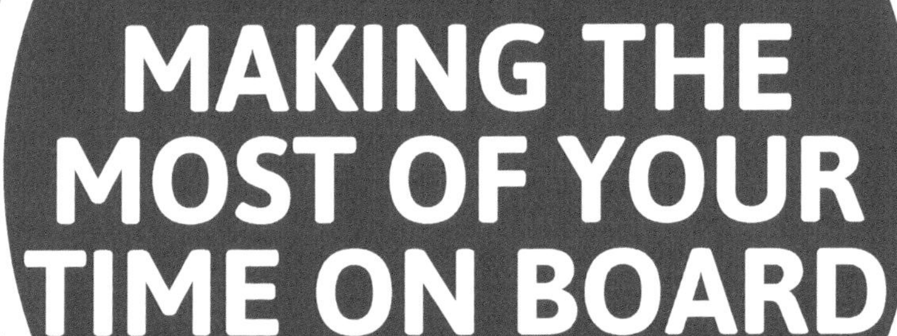

"It is better to travel well than to arrive"

Buddha

Queen Mary 2 docked in Saint Kitts.

Avoiding the Caribbean Blur

The couple at the table next to us was arguing about whether Saint Kitts was Saint Kitts, or if it was Saint Lucia or Saint Thomas. They had clearly been overcome with a dose of the 'Caribbean Blur'. The islands they had visited had all merged into one smudge of beautiful blue sea, sunny skies, and lush green hills. It is a terrible affliction that cruise passengers are very susceptible to catching.

Cruising around the Caribbean is an incredible experience. You gently slip into a new island every morning, and each seems to be more beautiful than the one you saw the day before. But, because they can seem similar on the surface, it's important to seek and explore the differences and diversity of each.

I like to seek and savor the special qualities of every place I visit, as I never know if I will have the privilege of seeing it again. I always arrive in a new destination with an understanding of the history, the culture, and the significant attractions. While I am there, I am an obsessive photo taker. I collect flyers and tickets, and make notes about what I see, taste, or smell to remind me of the things that made that place special and unique. While this approach to traveling works everywhere I go, I have found it is essential for traveling in the Caribbean.

When you have more time to spend on an island, you can slowly come to understand and appreciate its distinctiveness. The cruise experience does not make this easy as you only visit for a short time.

The history of the islands is broadly similar: English and French fighting over them, with the English dominating and driving out the Carib Indian locals to import slaves to build the sugar industry. While the popular tourist excursions touch on this story on the way to the beach or catamaran trip, not many focus on exploring the uniqueness of the culture, and the story of the people on each island.

There is no denying that a Caribbean cruise is a stunning experience. I adore the place. The islands are beautiful, the beaches and sea glorious, and the people on most of the islands are charming, welcoming, and surprisingly patient. It is even more fascinating when you escape from the tourist bubbles and standard experiences, and explore the culture at a deeper level.

The beach in Saint Kitts. The Caribbean is the most popular cruising destination in the world.

Embarkation Day Advice and Tips

Making the most of embarkation day is an essential part of ensuring a good start to your cruise vacation. The following is the process and routine I recommend for the day:

1. **Luggage:**
   - Make sure the luggage tags provided by the cruise line are secure on your cases, to ensure delivery to the correct cabin.
   - Pack your valuables, medication, documentation, and the other items I recommended in the Packing Advice and Tips section in your hand baggage.

2. **Check that you have your passport, or other required identification, and credit card:** Leaving passport or alternative identification at home is a common mistake. Even if you are traveling within a home region you may need your passport, as it is often the preferred form of identification.

3. **Allow a lot of time to ensure that you do not miss the ship:**
   - If you are flying to join a cruise, it is better to arrive the day before in case of a flight delay. It is especially important when not using cruise line-arranged flights, as they are unlikely to hold departure or get you to the first port of call if you miss it.
   - If driving to the ship, allow a lot of time for traffic problems. Have the cruise line emergency contact number on hand, in case you run late.

4. **Get to the port early, as you can often get on the ship earlier than the ticket indicates:** You can then explore the ship while it is still quiet. Once the ship starts to fill up during the afternoon, the elevators will be extremely busy, as some are used for luggage and others will be ferrying all the arrivals to their cabins.

5. **As soon as you board, find and check your cabin, and meet your steward:**
   - Report any defects or issues, so they can be dealt with before the rush.

- If you are unhappy with your cabin, you stand a greater chance of getting an alternative if you ask early.
- Discuss your preferences and likes with the steward.
- Check the safe works, and put all your valuables in it.
- Check the following information in the cabin:
  - Time and place of the safety drill, and the location of your life vests. Make a note of your muster station, and find it on your ship tour. The muster station is where you need to congregate if there is an emergency on board.
  - Your allocated restaurant and the number of your table. Visit the restaurant and check the table location, so you have time to ask for any changes.
  - Embarkation day special offers. There will usually be offers for Internet packages, spa treatments, and drink packages. Make a note of the ones that you want, and where to book them, and then do so as you take your tour of the ship.
  - Departure time and location of the sail-away party.

6. **Tour and familiarize yourself with the ship:** Spend the time before departure to get a feel for the layout, and where things are located. You should have a deck plan in the cabin. I recommend you head to the top deck, and then work your way down to the main lobby area.

7. **Have something to eat:** Most people head for the buffet restaurant on embarkation day, but usually the main restaurant is open and will be quieter and less frantic.

A selection of lunchtime desserts from the self-service buffet on the Silversea *Silver Whisper.*

No Ship, Six Passengers and the Mediterranean

Sherry Laskin blogs at CruiseMaven.com

I don't fly. Ever. In fact, I travel the world without flying. To do so, I spend an inordinate amount of time aboard cruise ships, shuttling between and throughout North America, the Caribbean, Europe, South America, and the South Pacific.

My complex trips are arranged like an elaborate array of dominoes. If one tile gets out of sync, the entire design comes to a standstill. If there was ever a failure in just one link of my grandiose travel plans, it could mean playing catch-up across continents to locate my cruise ship, riverboat, or train.

A couple of years ago I was headed to meet my ship in Marseille. This was my first Mediterranean cruise, and included a long-anticipated day in exotic Tunisia. After an exhausting two-week Atlantic crossing, two long trans-Europe train trips, questionable taxi drivers, and one motor coach, it was departure day in Marseille.

Only one problem: no ship. The cruise line did not notify me that the ship was unable to dock in Marseille due to high winds. Except for two security guards at the front entrance, I was alone inside the cavernous, steel-gray Marseille terminal. Neither guard knew if the ship was delayed, where it was, or what had happened to it.

Thirty minutes passed, and five more displaced passengers arrived, none of whom were aware of the ship's predicament. A desk phone rang, its tinny ring-ring reverberating through the empty terminal. A security guard answered it and, in his best English, informed us the ship had been forced to return to Toulon. Soon, he promised, a motor coach would arrive to take us on the 45 minute ride to Toulon.

Within an hour, the six of us were aboard the bus, snaking through the mountain pass to Toulon. As we turned onto a very narrow street along Toulon's historic waterfront, we caught sight of our ship, docked amid a marina full of sailboats, patiently waiting for us.

On the lowest deck, and parallel to the cement pier, a door was propped opened. There was no formal gangway to cross, just a very short metal ramp. Grabbing our elbows, two crew members quickly hoisted us aboard through the steel portal. As soon as both of my feet and three suitcases were safely on board, the heavy door slammed shut and within seconds we were underway, bound for North Africa.

On this trip, the frantic feeling of being unable to find my ship, and the desolation of being alone in a foreign city, had a bright side. I was able to experience an impromptu drive through a mountain range in France, and enjoy an unexpected tour of Toulon. Any seasoned traveler will tell you to 'roll with the punches'. My most important bit of advice as you journey on? Find the bright side. It's there. Sometimes, you just have to be patient until it appears.

Who Is Who On Board

In addition to sharing with you the key people who work to make sure of an unforgettable cruising experience, I have tips and advice on how to get the most out of them.

Captain

The Captain is responsible for the navigation and all on-board operations. He or she acts as the host and face of the cruise line, and you should see them frequently around the ship. They will host cocktail parties and often invite people to join them for dinner. You are unlikely to be invited onto the bridge to meet the Captain on passenger cruise ships, due to security requirements of the major cruise lines, but on freighters, river boats, and yachts, the Captain is likely to be willing for you to visit the bridge.

Chief Engineer

The Chief Engineer is responsible for maintaining the engines, and ensuring the ship has power to sail and to run all facilities. You are unlikely to see him or her other than at an official function such as the Captain's Cocktail party. If you are interested in the mechanical side of the ship, join one of the 'behind-the-scenes' tours, as you will then get to meet them to discuss the ship engineering.

Hotel Manager

The Hotel Manager has a vast role as every operation, except engineering and navigation, falls within their responsibility, including food and drink, housekeeping, and revenue-generating features such as the shops, excursions, and the casino. They are the person you should ask to see if you have a major issue with one of these areas, or if you have received remarkable service from someone.

Executive Chef

The Executive Chef is responsible for providing food for the passengers and crew on board. On large cruise ships, their department can be providing 20,000 meals a day. If the ship offers a 'behind-the-scenes' tour of the kitchens, they will usually lead the tour and share secrets and insights into the complex process of planning and preparing meals on ships. If it is not offered, speak to the Social Host or Purser, as Executive Chefs are very proud of their operations and will often provide tours for people who are really interested in the culinary side of cruising.

Cruise Director

The Cruise Director, sometimes known as the Entertainment Director, is responsible for the successful delivery of entertainment on the ship, and for keeping passengers busy. They plan the daily program of activities, and their team run the events. Getting to know them is the best way to get inside tips about the ship and the ports.

Social Host/Hostess

The Social Host/Hostess is responsible for managing key social events on board, including the Captain's cocktail parties, looking after the needs of VIP guests and hosting meet-ups for groups such as solo travelers. They also act as the cruise line family liaison if there is a death on board. On many lines they are the Captain's assistants, so building a good relationship with them can be the key to getting invited to events and meetings with the Captain.

Excursion Manager

The Excursion Manager is responsible for the sale, bookings, and delivery of the port-excursion program. They can provide insights into the best-rated and most popular tours, as they see all the ratings and comments left by previous guests. It is worth getting to know them, and asking their advice based on your interests.

Future Sales Manager

The Future Sales Manager is responsible for promoting and taking bookings for future cruises with the cruise line. As I covered in the fare section, they can usually offer you extra discounts for booking on board. Ask them about forthcoming promotions, and how full and busy future trips are, as this can give you insights on how flexible you need to be when booking.

Purser/Reception

The Purser/Reception Staff are responsible for answering ad-hoc questions from passengers, problem solving, and preparing bills. They also help with customs forms and preparing for and communicating the disembarkation process. This team is mostly on the receiving end of complaints, instead of being asked for advice and tips. Being friendly and building a good rapport with the team on the desk is a good idea, as they will go out of their way to help solve any issues you may have throughout your trip, and may even be willing to give extras, like early disembarkation passes.

Restaurant Maîitre d'

The Maître d's are responsible for managing the restaurants. They manage the table seating, the wait staff, and may also do some at-table preparation of food. Make a point of introducing yourself at the start of the cruise, to ensure they remember you, as it may prove invaluable if you have any concerns with your table companions or service later on.

Butler

The Butler is responsible for looking after the needs of premium-suite guests. This can include unpacking and packing, serving meals in the cabin, arranging reservations and excursion bookings, bringing evening canapés, replenishing the mini-bar, and organizing drink parties in the suite. They can problem-solve, and sort out many issues, so you should discuss with them anything you are trying to get resolved. They can suggest unusual and interesting places to visit or eat at in ports, based on feedback from previous passengers.

Cabin Steward

The Cabin Steward is responsible for keeping cabins clean and serviced. They check and service your cabin at least twice a day, including doing turndown service for non-suite cabins. They are very hardworking, and requests for things you like, such as additional towels, toiletries, or the way the bed is made, are usually well responded to.

Excursions in ports are an opportunity to try new experiences like riding quad bikes.

Activities, Meetings, and Clubs

The range of activities on a cruise depends on the type of cruise. There are some standard activities, meetings, and clubs you are likely to find on board:

- **Emergency drill:** The compulsory event that takes place before the ship departs. You are instructed on safety procedures and how to put on your life vests.
- **Sail-away parties:** These take place while leaving each port, usually out on deck. A chance to sell you cocktails, champagne, and drinks.
- **Captain's cocktail parties:** You can have a photograph taken with the Captain.
- **Cruise Critic meet-ups:** You sign up via the CruiseCritic.com site before sailing, so you can mingle with people you talked to online.
- **Solo traveler meet-ups:** Hosted meetings for independent travelers to meet each other and find partners to attend events and excursions.
- **'Friends of Dorothy' meet-ups**: These are for gay, lesbian, bi-sexual, and transgender travelers.
- **'Friends of Bill W' meet-ups:** These are for members of Alcoholics and Narcotics Anonymous, and operate as they would on land.
- **Art Auctions:** Selling art on ships is a big business, with regular exhibitions and auctions.
- **'Behind-the-Scenes' tours:** These occur on at-sea days, and take you on escorted tours of the kitchens and other ship facilities.
- **Entertainment:** Here are the main types of entertainment you will find on a cruise ship:
  - Dance classes, exhibitions and balls.
  - Trivia and quizzes.
  - Bingo and casino.
  - Live music and bands in the lounges and bars.
  - Production or featured artist shows in the show lounge.
  - Passenger talent shows and karaoke.
  - Enlightenment and port lectures.
  - Interdenominational religious services.
  - Shopping promotions: perfume, watches, jewelry, branded merchandise, and alcohol.
  - Demonstrations by on-board departments, such as flower arranging and cooking.

Sunning and swimming on deck in the Mediterranean.

Bridge, Spinning, and Soufflés

Mark Sanford is my partner and fellow traveler.

I used to come back from my vacations with souvenirs and photographs. Now I come back with new skills.

I love the experience of cruising, of slicing through the sea, the amazing food, the kaleidoscope of destinations, and the mixture of people I get to meet. But one of the underrated aspects of cruising I have come to treasure is the classes, talks, and demonstrations laid on to entertain and inform guests.

The first skill I learned while cruising was how to play bridge. It was something I had been meaning to do for years, but never found the time. On a crossing of the Atlantic, I joined a morning class after breakfast, with a group of other passengers. It was a friendly cross-generational group. As the sea churned past the windows of the card room, we mastered the game over the six days at sea.

I also learned how to 'spin'. I had wanted to try out cycling spin classes at my local gym, but had never plucked up the courage to join the lycra-clad demons attacking the bikes. They all seemed to know exactly what to do, and I was nervous about stepping into the class as a newbie and looking foolish. The classes offered on board my cruise around the Mediterranean felt much less risky. I discovered my inner lycra, and a passion for cycling and spinning.

Thanks to cruising, soufflés are now part of my cooking repertoire. The chefs often run demonstrations and share recipes for some of the popular dishes on board. My sweet tooth drew me to this particular experience, and I have now mastered the art of making this challenging dessert, thanks to their skills.

Sometimes what I learn is a bit of fun trivia. Thanks to a series of talks on a cruise by the actress Celia Imrie, I also learned how television shows are commissioned and produced. This actress is a major television star in the UK, and appeared in films such as *Calendar Girls.*

On the last cruise we went on, there was an ice sculpting demonstration. Now that would be one impressive skill to come home with! Maybe next time.

Cruise ships often have large and busy gyms to burn off all those extra calories. This is the *MSC Preziosa* gym.

Shore Excursions: Exploring the Options 

The natural tendency is to book excursions through your cruise line. If none appeal, or cruisers are looking to save money, they default to the 'do your own thing' option, which means catching the shuttle bus or walking into the town and strolling about. However, there is a third and underused option, which is to go on an excursion provided by independent operators. They are usually a cheaper option, and also support the local economy.

There are many advantages of going on shore excursions offered by independent operators:

- You will get the same tour as those offered by the cruise line, but for less money.
- The same tour will have fewer people on it.
- There will be spaces available on popular tours that are sold out via your cruise line.
- Specialty tours will be offered that are not available through the cruise line, including sporting activities, history, food, or art.
- You can read reviews and see photos from passengers who took the tours.
- You will depart and return to ship side, as the cruise line tours do.
- Most will guarantee to get you back to the ship before departure, or will get you to the next port if you do miss the ship.

How to find the best cruise port excursions

To ensure the alternative tour you choose is well organized, and good quality, take these steps:

- Check how many ships will be in port to help guide your excursion choice. Use a site such as CruiseTimetables.com to see how busy a port will be when you are there. For example, I noted there were going to be seven ships in Saint Thomas on Boxing Day. With 15,000 passengers in the port, we booked an all-day excursion on a boat instead, stopping at remote beaches to avoid crowded attractions.

- Check what excursions, prices, and availability your cruise line has. Cruise lines usually have an online cruise personalizer, where you can book excursions from 90 days before your cruise departs. You should access it early, as many popular tours sell out.
- Decide if any of your cruise line's excursions appeal, and note the prices and availability.
- Review and compare options on the various independent shore excursion sites. There are a number of sites such as Viator.com, ShoreTrips.com, and CruisingExcursions.com that specialize in providing excursions for cruise line passengers. They allow you to input your cruise line, ship, and departure date, and then show all your port stops along with the available excursions.

While I often end up using the cruise line options because they are convenient, independent excursions are an excellent way to save money and enjoy a unique experience.

The Church of Spilt Blood in Saint Petersburg, Russia. Cruise ships spend two or three days here when they visit this incredible city.

My Cycling Revelation: Learning and Burning Calories

Going on a cycling tour while on a cruise makes me feel virtuous. I convince myself I am burning off the excess calories from the scrumptious desserts that I am succumbing to at both lunch and dinner. Of course, I know the exercise from the two- or three-hour tour makes little impact on my indulgences, but it is a remarkable way to see, understand, and feel a destination.

This revelation came to me when I went on my first cycling tour on a stop in Saint Kitts, in the Caribbean. We chose the tour simply because the others sounded so mundane. The cycling tour promised a mixture of sightseeing, exploration of the history of the island's sugar industry, and time to swim at one of the remote beaches. It sounded like a perfect mix of exercise, relaxation, and insights.

The tour was led by a local man, whose family could be traced back to the days of slavery, and by a chirpy English man who had adopted Saint Kitts as his home for more than 20 years. Both adored the island as if it was their child, and relished showing us around. Their enthusiasm was impressive, considering they do the same tour every day for at least six months of the year.

The more we asked, the more animated they got and the more we were shown. We wended through villages as they pointed out where their friends and family lived, and told us stories of the local lifestyle and how they earn a living. They took us to the ruins of old sugar estate houses and refineries, and told us how almost overnight the sugar industry collapsed and the island had to find new ways to create employment and make money. They proudly toured us past the massive runway, screaming excitedly, and got us to wave at Kim Collins, the world champion runner who represented Saint Kitts in the Olympics four times, as he drove past in his car.

Finally, we pulled into a secluded beach that tourists would never usually find, for a swim in the beautiful Caribbean Sea, while being served rum punch and soft drinks. It was a memorable day. It got me hooked on cycling as a way to see a destination

I have cycled up steep stone pathways in Madeira to get to vantage points looking across the Atlantic Ocean. I have toured the suburbs and the crumbling castle defenses in Saint Maarten, while the Dutch and French guides told us that the island is the smallest landmass in the world with two countries on it. I have cycled along winding roads to find out-of-the-way beaches away from the crush of tourists in Sardinia.

The experiences are so much more vivid and insightful when gained through the informality of a cycling tour. The first thing I do when I get the excursion list for a cruise is to scan it for cycling tours. If none are listed, I go online to see what independent providers offer. Learning while burning calories is a great combination.

Other Tips for Your Time On Board

Over the years that I have been cruising, I have developed a few general tips to help travelers ensure they make the most of time on board.

Treat your cruise card as cash, and track your spending.

The cruise card you are given on check-in is your ID, room key, and charge card for everything you buy on board. Watch out for spending more than you planned. Every few days, get a printout of your bill from reception, and monitor it against your budget. Some cruise lines offer the option of checking your bill on your television in your cabin.

Don't over-schedule and commit in advance to tours every day.

The ship is a destination in its own right, so plan time to explore and enjoy the facilities. The best time to do that is when everyone else has gone on shore excursions. The ship is quiet and calm, and you will find places less crowded. There are usually special offers and discounts during these times in places such as the spa.

Use the daily program to plan your day.

Cruise lines schedule multiple activities for every hour of every day. The choice is large, even before you overlay personal activities such as reading, going to the gym, swimming, or going to the spa. Each night, before you go to bed, go through the daily program and plan the next day.

If you have a set dining room and time, request the biggest table option.

The largest table on cruise ships is for eight passengers. Sitting there means you will meet a diverse group of people, and you will likely click with at least some of your tablemates. If you are at a table with just one other couple and do not 'click', it will make meals a chore instead of a pleasure. If you want a table for two people, make sure you request it early, as availability is limited.

Give a gratuity or welcome gift up front to your cabin steward.

Even if your fare includes tips, giving a small cash gratuity, gift, or some treat from home is usually welcome, and helps ensure a good rapport and extra care and attention from these busy members of staff.

Hold back on shopping.
Do not buy things from the on-board shops at the start of your cruise – wait for the daily promotions to start. Cruise lines run promotions and events, offering large discounts on specific merchandise sectors each day. When in port, especially in the Caribbean, it's easy to get carried away with the promise of duty- and tax-free shopping. You will be offered incentives, such as free earrings and charms for bracelets, to get you into the stores. Staff are highly trained and experienced in making sales of luxury goods, diamonds, and watches, to cruise passengers.

Plan for and use self-disembarkation.
If you have controlled your packing and resisted the temptation to buy large souvenirs in every port, then apply to self-disembark the ship. This means you will usually be able to get off the ship within an hour of docking, as soon as the port authorities and immigration officials have cleared the ship to disembark passengers. If you cannot carry your luggage to self-disembark, book an early transfer through the cruise. This will come with a scheduled time to disembark to meet your transfer.

Celebrity Cruises coming in to dock in Dominica.

BEING A RESPONSIBLE CRUISER

*"The traveler sees what he sees,
the tourist sees what he has come to see"*

Gilbert K. Chesterton

The Hidden Ship

It is rare for passengers to be allowed to explore behind the doors marked 'Crew Only'. When I did this on the *Queen Elizabeth*, I felt as dazed and bewildered as the children in *The Lion, the Witch and the Wardrobe*, when they found themselves in a totally different and alien world a few paces through the back of the cupboard. In just a few steps I was transported into a totally different ship.

Passengers occupy the outside surface and skin of a ship, and walk past the numerous doors that sweep the crew from this pampered world into another realm secreted within the ship.

As you step through one of those doors you abruptly leave behind luxury and step into a metallic and functional world. It occupies at least as much space as that used by passengers, but there are no thick carpets, no decorated walls, and no drapes to soften the look and absorb the noise. It is an echoing and clattering space that operates as a sprawling, self-sufficient city.

The ship carries crew in similar numbers to passengers to serve their needs and operate the ship. The crew also needs places to live, relax, and work. There are vast kitchens to prepare food, places to store all the ingredients and supplies for the cruise, laundry facilities, water purification plants, electric generation plants, recycling plants, printing presses, firefighting equipment, a hospital, and everything you can think of that a city needs to operate.

When I went on my first tour, I realized I had never thought properly about just how much has to go on behind the scenes to keep a ship operating.

Running through the *Queen Elizabeth* is a long passageway, known as 'Main Road'. It runs from the ship's bow to the stern, to get the crew and supplies to any place in the ship as quickly as possible. Crew rush along it, joining the flow as they clatter down the stairs to use the throughway to access another part of the ship to fetch something, and clattering back up the stairs, to return to the world the passengers live in, once they have retrieved it.

Ever since that exploration of the ship-within-the-ship, I have had a new appreciation for cruising. I had taken for granted all the basics such as lights, water, and heat, not really thinking that, while out at sea or cruising along rivers, the ships have to produce everything that is needed. It's obvious when you think about it, but I had never contemplated the scale and logistics of managing a cruise. Imagine trying to order accurate quantities of ingredients to make and serve thousands of meals every day for a week, or ensuring enough generated power to provide lights and heat, and operate all the ship's equipment, from ovens to water purifiers to toilets.

Every time I look at a ship, I now think about the ship within it. I like to think about how we, as passengers, live on the surface of a remarkable sailing city, taking for granted the things we do not see.

Indoor pools, like this one on *MSC Preziosa* are popular with families in all weather.

Understanding that All Is Not Perfect

Over the years, as I have gained a better understanding of the impact the cruising industry has on the people that work in it, the environment, and the regions of the world it visits, I have realized that cruising is not perfect. It has flaws and areas that can be improved, but I believe that if passengers make subtle changes in the way that we think and act, we can help make cruising an even safer, more respectful, and responsible way to travel.

I have some principles that I apply to all my cruise journeys to help me to be more respectful, more responsible, and safer.

When I first got into cruising, I developed an overly optimistic view of it. This came from devouring books with glowing stories about the grand icons of the heyday of transatlantic crossings, such as the *Titanic, Lusitania,* and the 'Queens' (*Queen Mary and Queen Elizabeth*). The books I read were upbeat and positive reflections written by maritime historians and people who love ships[5]. They left me convinced that cruising was glamorous, exciting, and perfect.

I learned about the complex politics behind ships, and how European governments had helped fund them as icons of national pride, and as potential troop carriers in case of war. I read stories of the rich and famous traveling in the gilded First Class, and of the optimistic immigrants crammed into Steerage, dreaming of new opportunities by escaping from Europe. I discovered how the transatlantic business imploded when scheduled jet flights slashed the time of the crossing from days to hours.

I was enthralled by how sailing on cruise ships languished as a niche habit until 1972[6], when Ted Arison developed Caribbean cruises out of Miami on the cheap, fun ships of the Carnival line. It was interesting to read about the development of modern cruising as Carnival and its arch-rival Royal Caribbean fought to win passengers by investing in ships and constantly promoting cruising.

My early reading left me with a glowing and positive impression of everything about cruising. Then I read two books that challenged my perspective, and played a role in informing and guiding the way I now behave when on ship: *Cruise Ship Blues*[7]*: The Underside of the Cruise Ship Industry* and *Cruise Ship Squeeze: The New Pirates of the Seven Seas*[8], both by Ross A. Klein.

Although many cruise fans, and the industry, feel the books are unfair and overly critical, they made me stop and think. They encouraged me to reflect on the negative impact that the rapid growth in cruising may be having on the people that work in the field, the places they visit, and the environment. In his books he argues that a) the cruise industry registers ships in countries with less stringent labor laws in order to exploit the work force, b) they do not push much economic benefit into the regions they call on, as they control the excursions and source all their food and supplies in their home ports, and c) the ships are poor for the environment.

While Klein takes an overly pessimistic view, reading his books was a significant trigger for me. They helped me to shape how I think and act as a cruiser, and inspired me to become a more responsible and respectful traveler. They encouraged me to think beyond the surface of my experience, to the incredible service and pleasure I get from being on board a ship, and to think about how even small actions I take could have a positive impact on the people that work on ships, my fellow passengers, the places we visit, and the environment. They are not massive and difficult actions, but steps that I believe everyone cruising should take to make it a safer, more respectful and responsible way to travel.

The Royal Caribbean ship, *Brilliance of the Seas,* moored in Geiranger, Norway.

A Star in the Making

I met Hal Smith on his very first cruise. He had never wanted to go on one before. Hal and his wife, Meg, are from Springfield, Illinois, and were fellow passengers on a Baltic cruise on Silversea's *Silver Whisper*.

When I asked Hal what the star attraction of the cruise was, it was not the three million priceless artworks in the Hermitage in Saint Petersburg, nor the cathedrals and historic buildings of Tallinn or Helsinki. It was watching his daughter, Elizabeth, perform in the theatre every night. She was the reason he finally agreed to his wife's request to try out cruising.

Elizabeth was one of the six singers that entertained the guests each night in the ship's theatre.

Since the age of five, Elizabeth Smith has put on shows for her family. She would belt out songs her parents loved so much they had them on 'repeat' on their CD player. Songs such as 'I Say A Little Prayer', 'It's My Party And I'll Cry If I Want To', and 'Diamonds Are A Girl's Best Friend'. With her parents on board, Elizabeth arranged to perform a cabaret show called 'Here I Am', with those same songs. It was fabulous as it came from the heart, was authentic and warm. It was hard to tell if the Smiths or the rest of the passengers loved it more.

Meeting Hal, Meg and Elizabeth brought home to me the role that cruise lines play in providing a training ground for up and coming artists. As the ships work their way around the world, they carry young, talented and ambitious actors, dancers and singers who have studied their art at college, and are now desperate to fine-tune their skills. Working on a ship gives them the ability to perform in front of large audiences every night, and get constant feedback. They can hone their skills and learn.

Elizabeth's ambition is to build a career in television, and her work on the ship has started to open doors. Based on the enthusiasm, determination and skill I observed, I am sure one day I will be able to say I met and got to know Elizabeth Smith and her parents on a cruise before she was a household name.

Being Respectful

Respect the sea

Every Captain I have interviewed on my travels talks about how they instill in their crew the importance of respecting the sea. Passengers need to do this as well.

There are a few ways that we can help:

- Never throw anything over the side of the ship.
- Minimize waste, including the use of water, as everything has to be processed on board and, based on what it is, either disposed of into the sea, or offloaded in ports.
- Choose cruise lines that have clear environmental policies, and awards for environmental good practice beyond the minimum required by law. Cruise lines have to meet international environmental regulations, such as what they can discharge into the sea, recycling, and the use of certain types of fuel when they are in port or cruising in some regions of the world. For example, cruise lines use fuel with lower emissions in the Norwegian Fjords to meet Norway's environmental requirements.

Respect the crew

Most cruise lines sail under flags of convenience that allow them to apply the laws and regulations of the country their cruise ship is registered in, not the home country of the cruise company. This helps reduce costs to meet demand for low cruise fares, but it also means they do not have to comply with regulations regarding things such as minimum wages and working hours that apply in their home market.

Crews work on contracts of three to nine months at a time, seven days a week, with long hours each day. It is demanding and tough, even more so as they have to be friendly, cheerful, and helpful at all times. They are the interface for the cruise line and passengers, and really make our experience.

Despite this, staff retention levels are high. However, most crew members have to be recruited from emerging markets, as the take-home wages (even after taking account of the free board and food) can be below the minimum wage, or what would be seen as acceptable for the work, in more affluent western countries.

There are ways you can help the crew:

- Don't remove gratuities auto-added to your bill. It ensures everyone is paying into the pot, and the crew is benefiting.
- Tip great service, even if the cruise fare covers gratuities. You will not miss the few extra dollars, but it will add up to a meaningful amount for the crew across a contract period.
- Reward good service by completing the recognition cards, mentioning staff members by name on cruise evaluation forms, or speaking to the Head of Department. Most cruise lines have Employee of the Month and other recognition awards. These recommendations may be taken into account when staff promotions are considered.
- Think about things to help reduce workload. These are small adjustments for us, but magnified across all the people the crew looks after, they will make a significant difference. This includes keeping cabins tidy and clean, and self-disembarking to reduce the crew workload on the hectic changeover days.

Being Responsible

It's important to be responsible towards local economies in ports you visit. Many of the popular destinations on cruise itineraries are in areas of poverty, with poor conditions among the local population. In my view, we should be ensuring that our actions before and during our visit are aimed at getting as much of our fare and expenditures into the hands of the local economy.

Here's how we can help:

- Visit destinations that are less developed and mass tourism-focused, where there are more local businesses and independent providers, rather than international chains.
- Do more self-led tours where you hire local taxi drivers and tour guides.
- Make a point of visiting local shops and markets, instead of the chain stores in the port-side malls.

Be responsible towards your fellow passengers and crew by not bringing illness – such as norovirus – on board with you. Cruise lines cannot prevent it being brought on board, and they rely on passengers to be honest.

If there is an outbreak, it creates an enormous amount of extra duties for the crew, on top of their existing responsibilities. I have been on a ship where there was an outbreak. The key reason it spread was that passengers followed neither the advice on sanitization, nor the quarantine requirements after contracting the virus.

Here are some ways that we can help:

- Be honest when completing the declaration before boarding, even if it means you may be quarantined for the first day of your cruise.
- Wash hands with soap and water regularly, and use the anti-bacterial gel placed around the ship.
- Report symptoms immediately to the medical team. They may ask you to stay in your cabin for 24 to 48 hours to ensure you are all healthy.
- Follow the guidelines and stay in your cabin if you contract a virus.

Being Safe

Just because we are staying in a contained environment, surrounded by other people, lots of crew, and security, does not mean everyone is honest or that something bad cannot happen. Because we are heading off on escorted excursions with other people in beautiful and interesting places of the world, does not mean crime does not exist. We need to retain our common sense and be as careful as we would at home or on any other vacation.

You can check on the incidence of cruise accidents through the United States Coast Guard site. It reports all incidents for lines operating out of the United States, including accidents, suspicious deaths, assaults, and sexual assaults. The website CruiseJunkie.com tracks every incident, globally, and is currently the most comprehensive resource available. Following pressure by the United

States government, changes are being proposed as to the collection and reporting of information about shipboard accidents and incidents. There will be more transparency and consistency in reporting, and shipping lines will be displaying more data on their websites, for passenger review.

Accidents

If you are concerned about accidents, I recommend the following:

- If you fear being stranded far from land, then consider river or barge cruising to build your confidence. The ships travel close to land and if there is an incident you will be in sight of and in easy reach of land.
- If you are concerned about insufficient and inadequate equipment, remember that cruise lines have to comply with laws laid out by the International Maritime Organization. This includes the 1974 International Convention for the Safety of Life at Sea (SOLAS) regulations[9], which requires all ships to have sufficient lifeboats, life jackets, emergency equipment, and personnel trained to tackle any major incidents. However, you may prefer to cruise on only the newest ships, as they will have the latest equipment and be designed to address any lessons learned from previous incidents.

Should an incident occur at sea, follow the crew's instructions without delay and get to your muster station as promptly as possible.

Personal Safety

These are some of the things we should do to ensure our personal safety:

- Muster drills. Attend them and pay careful attention. These are where the Captain runs through the safety procedures, and you are taught how to put on your life vest. He advises what to do in an emergency, what you need to bring if you are called to your muster station, and the specific ship's safety regulations.
- Smoking. Fire at sea is the incident ships dread – they can spread fast and are hard to control. Ships have restrictions on where you can smoke. If you do smoke, make sure your cigarettes are completely out, and never throw butts over the side of the ship as they can be drawn back into the ship and start a fire.

- Balconies and handrails. Every year, people fall off ships and are lost at sea. Never sit on balcony handrails, and make sure your children are aware of the danger, and watch them carefully.
- Think about security on board:
  - Bring as few valuables as you can, and keep them locked in your safe.
  - The main safety issues on a ship are the same crimes that occur on land, such as thefts and assaults. So act as you would at home to prevent these sorts of crimes.
- Be especially careful and aware in port:
  - Do not take valuables or a lot of cash with you.
  - Take some photo identification (not your passport), and the emergency number for the handling agent in the port.
  - Stick with the crowds, go on escorted excursions, and only use taxis from the official ranks.
  - Remember that places you visit may be poor, and wealthy cruise passengers can be seen as easy targets, relaxed and off-guard.

If you are unfortunate enough to be affected by an incident, contact the ship's security team immediately. Ask for documentation of your report, and contact your insurance company as soon as possible.

The Medina market in the old town of Tunis, which I visited on *MSC Preziosa's* maiden voyage.

The Quirky Couple and the Night Butler

My first vacation on a ship was a stormy winter transatlantic crossing on Cunard's *Queen Elizabeth 2* from Southampton to New York; the ship was starting a new world cruise. My suite was high up on the Penthouse Deck, and I was thrilled, as I knew that a few doors down from us would be the Cunard Cruise Line's most important passengers. I had read about them in various articles, and on cruise message boards online, and I was excited to get to observe the quirky and opulent world they inhabited.

Although the *QE2* constantly ferried famous celebrities across the Atlantic and around the world, a retired financier and his wife were the ship's most infamous passengers. This fabulously wealthy couple annually cruised around the world for at least three months, booking the two most expensive suites and often several other premium cabins close by. One suite was used to sleep in, one to entertain in, and the others used to store the clothes, accessories and other goods they brought on board for the trip.

During our crossing of the Atlantic, I saw trunks being hauled up onto our deck and maneuvered into one of the suites. The butlers told us these trunks would be full of clothes or other items the couple decided were needed. They hinted the couple permanently stored jewelry on board to avoid the need to pack and bring it along each year. Often, their table in the dining room would be covered in small Disney characters, as the couple were known to be massive fans and would bring some of their collection on board.

Each evening, before dinner, they would sit in the lounge in front of the restaurant, smoking while having cocktails. During dinner, the couple would carry on smoking. They were so important to the cruise line that even as smoking was being banned elsewhere on ships it was still allowed in this dining room. As they returned to their suite after dinner, they would signal for the night butler to bring them their usual evening dish of raspberries.

The night butler was a woman named Sheila. She had worked on the ship for at least 20 years, and only worked at night. She inhabited a small kitchen at the top of the stairs, and was there to ensure that this couple and other guests on the deck were attended to through the night. As you headed back to the cabin at night, she would leap out excitedly, chat and bustle about preparing your usual drinks and bedtime treat.

The retirement of the *QE2* after 40 years at sea brought an end to the on-going journeys by this fascinating couple and Sheila. I understand the couple refused to move to the newer *Queen Mary 2* as smoking was to be banned, and there was no role for a dedicated night butler. I believe the retirement of the ship also signaled something more significant in the history of cruising. The *QE2* was the last of the old-style liners, with its unique design, and free flowing and tailored style to serving guests like that quirky couple. As cruising becomes more mainstream, and tries to be more affordable and accessible, it is being replaced with a more corporate approach, which includes harmonious ship layouts and designs, more rigorous guidelines and rules, and stricter cost controls. Perhaps risking the loss of some of its former color and uniqueness in the process.

Final Thought

As cruise travel becomes more popular, I believe passengers have an important role to play. They must ensure the industry acts in a responsible and caring way towards the environment, the destinations, and the people who work within the field. Our obsession with low prices needs to be balanced with an expectation that good practices have associated costs.

By taking a longer-term view of what we want cruising to contribute to society – beyond a good value vacation – we can make a difference. I do not believe this will take a lot of effort on our part. It is about asking the challenging questions about safety and care, and choosing and rewarding providers that show they are driven as much by the values of responsibility, respect, and safety as they are by profits.

I love cruising and want everyone to try it at least once. I passionately believe there is a cruising option for everyone. Every single person can have an unforgettable time and will want to experience more. I just do not want it to come at an unnecessary cost to the world around us.

The *Royal Clipper* tall ship viewed from a beach in the Caribbean.

RESOURCES

The Traveler's Handbooks Series

- *The Adventure Traveler's Handbook*, by Nellie Huang
- *The Career Break Traveler's Handbook*, by Jeffrey Jung
- *The Family Traveler's Handbook*, by Mara Gorman
- *The Food Traveler's Handbook*, by Jodi Ettenberg
- *The Luxury Traveler's Handbook*, by Sarah & Terry Lee
- *The Solo Traveler's Handbook*, by Janice Leith Waugh
- *The Volunteer Traveler's Handbook*, by Shannon O'Donnell

Cruising Related Books

- *Berlitz Complete Guide to Cruising and Cruise Ships*, by Douglas Ward
- *Cruise Ship Blues: The Underside of the Cruise Industry,* by Ross A Klein
- *Cruise Ship Squeeze: The New Pirates of the Seven Seas*, by Ross A Klein

Cruise Magazines

- Porthole.com
- CruiseTravelMag.com
- Cruise-International.com
- WorldofCruising.co.uk

Industry Resources

- Cruising.org
- DiscoverCruises.co.uk
- IMO.org
- CruiseMarketWatch.com
- United States Coast Guard Cruise Line Incident Reporting Statistics: uscg.mil/hq/cg2/cgis/CruiseLine.asp

Community and Review Sites

- CruiseCritic.com
- CruiseMates.com
- CruisingMates.co.uk
- CruiselineFans.com
- CruiseHive.com
- CruiseCrazies.com
- Cruiseline.com
- CruiseMinded.com

Planning Resources and Tools

- ThemeCruiseFinder.com
- CruiseFareMonitor.com
- Cruisetip.tpkeller.com (On board tipping calculator)
- SpecialNeedsAtSea.com
- MobilityAtSea.co.uk
- CruiseTimetables.com
- ShoreExcursions.viator.com
- ShoreTrips.com
- CruisingExcursions.com

Cruise Lines

Passenger Cruise Lines (Large and Medium Ships)

- Carnival.com
- RoyalCaribbean.com
- NCL.com
- MSCCruises.com
- CostaCruise.com

- Princess.com
- CelebrityCruises.com
- HollandAmerica.com
- AIDA.de
- DisneyCruise.disney.go.com
- Cunard.com
- POCruises.com
- AtlantisEvents.com

Passenger Cruise Lines (Small and Boutique Ships)

- Silversea.com
- Seabourn.com
- RSSC.com
- CrystalCruises.com

Explorer and Adventure Lines

- RMS-St-Helena.com
- Hebridean.co.uk
- QuarkExpeditions.com
- HL-cruises.com
- Hurtigruten.com
- Expeditions.com
- Noble-Caledonia.co.uk

Tall Ships

- WindstarCruises.com
- StarClippers.com
- IslandWindjammers.com

Freighters

- FreighterCruises.com
- Cross-ocean.com
- FreighterTravel.co.nz

Yachts

- Seadream.com
- VarietyCruises.com

River Cruise Lines

- VikingRiverCruises.com
- Uniworld.com
- AmaWaterways.com
- ZambeziQueen.com
- AquaExpeditions.com
- AmericanQueenSteamboatCompany.com
- AmericanCruiseLines.com

Barges

- BargeCompany.com
- GoBarging.com
- WaterwaysHolidays.com

Residences at Sea

- AboardTheWorld.com

Learning at Sea

- SemesterAtSea.org
- UniversityAtSea.com

Docked Ships

- QueenMary.com
- SSRotterdam.nl/uk
- QE2hotels.com

Cruise Apps, Blogs, and Podcasts

Apps:

- ShipMateApp.com
- CruiseCardControl.com
- iCruise.com/iphoneapp
- DeckDirector.com

Blogs and Sites:

- TipsForTravellers.com/Cruising
- AvidCruiser.com
- GoCruiseWithJane.co.uk
- CruiseMiss.com
- CruiseCurrents.com
- CruiseMaven.com
- ChrisCruises.com
- CaptainGreyBeard.com
- ExpertCruiser.com
- Cruise-Dude.com
- CruiseDiva.com
- CruiseMeet.co.uk
- FamilyCruiseAdvisor.com
- EmmaOnBoard.com
- ChrisCunard.com
- CruiseLawNews.com (reports on incidents and legal issues)
- CruiseShipNorovirus.com (tracks incidence of norovirus)
- CruiseJunkie.com (tracks incidents and accidents)

Podcasts

- CruiseRadio.net
- CruizeCast.com

Endnotes

[1] Dimenhydrinate, Wikipedia.org, en.wikipedia.org/wiki/Dimenhydrinate

[2] Cinnarizine, Wikipedia.org, en.wikipedia.org/wiki/Cinnarizine

[3] Costa Concordia, Costa Concordia Disaster, BBC, bbc.co.uk/news/world-europe-16646686. 2013.

[4] Cruise Lines International Association (CLIA), Passenger Bill of Rights, http://www.cruising.org/issues-facts/safety-and-security/cruise-industry-passenger-bill-rights. 2013.

[5] Maxtone-Graham, John. *The Only Way To Cross*. Macmillian Publishing Company, 1978.

[6] Carnival Corporation & PLC, Wikipedia.org, en.wikipedia.org/wiki/Carnival_Corporation_%26_plc

[7] Klein, Ross A, *Cruise Ship Blues: The Underside of the Cruise Industry*. New Society Publishers. 2003.

[8] Klein, Ross A. *Cruise Ship Squeeze: The New Pirates of the Seven Seas*. New Society Publishers. 2005.

[9] International Maritime Organization, International Convention for the Safety of Life at Sea (SOLAS), imo.org/About/Conventions/ListOfConventions/Pages/International-Convention-for-the-Safety-of-Life-at-Sea-(SOLAS),-1974.aspx

Gary Bembridge has been an avid cruise fan and self-confessed ship geek for over a decade. He stumbled into cruising when he reluctantly went to a business conference taking part on a ship, and discovered he loved being at sea. Since then he has cruised extensively around the world. In addition to being a global marketing consultant, he also runs Tips for Travellers (TipsForTravellers.com) which he launched in 2005. There he podcasts, blogs and produces videos about travel and his first love: cruising.

The Cruise Traveler's Handbook

Gary Bembridge

Lightning Source UK Ltd.
Milton Keynes UK
UKIC01n1527051213
222462UK00001B/4